TERMINAL TALES

Memories of a
Rock Island
Chicago Division Trainmaster

1961-1964
by
J. Pete Hedgpeth

Published by C.P.M. –
Circulation, Publishing and Marketing L.L.C.
The Railway Book People
P.O. Box 941
Newton, IA 50208-0941

www.rybooks.com

Printed in the United States of America
Acid Free Paper
1st Edition, 2nd Printing

ISBN 192855106-8
Library of Congress Catalog Number 2003110346

Contents

DEDICATION

As I thought about a dedication page for this book, several names and groups of names came to mind. Throughout my Rock Island years close associations were formed as well as more distant relationships. During the Chicago Division years (1961-64) there were those with whom contact was daily and some with whom I only occasionally crossed paths.

When dedicating a book, it seems that considerable emphasis should be directed toward those with whom the writer had an ongoing and pleasurable relationship...those who shared the struggle, which at times seemed without end.

Therefore I have chosen to select the names of some of my favorite people who were in the trenches along with me. Both in "management" and "from the ranks". These guys were always there...putting in "supererogatory" effort day by day. Often knowing that no matter what...criticism was likely to be the upshot of the effort. Nonetheless we all carried on to the best of our ability.

Therefore here's the roster of "the good guys"..men who got the job done, without complaint and without close supervision.

At Joliet: these guys get the Gold Stars: Yardmaster Joe Van Gampler, Yard Clerk Bob Meysemberg, Switchmen "Pinky" Rogers, Dick Doolin and Ed Sealy. Towerman, Cliff Witherspoon also qualifies..in spite of his idiosyncrasies and inflated sense of his own importance, he got the job done.

At Blue Island-Chicago: Ralph Parker, Trainmaster who protected the other trainmasters from George to the extent of his ability. Fellow Trainmasters Frank Vestal and Cliff Brogden shared the duty day and night, continually fighting the battle with the switchmen below and George above. Yardmasters Mel Voitik who "got it done every night" in spite of everything that could go wrong went wrong, Al Simnick who, in a quiet unassuming way kept things moving and was respected by those he supervised.

Leonard Ellul who provided comic relief where ever he was working. He along with Mel Voitik who dared to call GHV "George" and never were intimidated by his harangues. There were some good guy switchmen too: Warren Anderson on the 47th St. Transfer who often handled the piggybacks. Warren also introduced me to Maxwell Street and the delectable Polish Sausage Sandwiches with hot peppers which we often indulged in before the first "pig run" on Saturday nights.

Well, there're probably more I haven't mentioned who are deserving, and some whom I can picture and remember in "mind's eye", but can't call by name, but this is a representative grouping of Rock Island men, who depended on her paychecks, but gave full measure of service in return.

Thanks to all of these fellow-employees and others who have contributed to "What I remember with Delight". You served your company well.

J. Pete Hedgpeth

Photo credits: All photographs except the following came from *The Rocket*, the Rock Island employees magazine. Cover design: John Nelson with background from the Chicago Tribune; John Nelson: p. 15 pass, p. 40; J. Pete Hedgpeth: pgs: 53, 99, 114, back cover; Dave Willett: p. 49; Pullman Standard Library, Vol 8, Randall and Anderson (attempts to contact this publisher were unsuccessful) p.11

Cover: Geep 1281 finds itself in the pit in this 1950's photograph. The fellow in the suit is believed to be Master Mechanic C.H. (Clarence) Gray and Blue Island Rip Track foreman Joe Salapatek.

INTRODUCTION

WHAT WE ENDURE WITH HARDSHIP, WE REMEMBER WITH DELIGHT "Traveling Op", Part 3 RAILROAD April 1947

About 12 years ago, or thereabouts, after hearing one of my "Stories" for the 12th time, the editor of our Lincoln Railfans Club Newsletter, said..."Why don't you start writing about your railroad memories and experiences? We can run it each month in the newsletter."

Well, being unable to think of any reason not to do it, I started a monthly piece which I originally called *ROCK ISLAND RAMBLINGS.* This went on for a year or two and then "one thing led to another" and I started to think about my experiences on the CB&Q as a brakeman in the 1950's right here on the Lincoln and Wymore Divisions in Nebraska.

Since I couldn't continue to call it ROCK ISLAND RAMBLINGS when I was writing about the CB&Q, I started to think about another, more all encompassing, name for my little column. Being a long time reader of RAILROAD MAGAZINE (I bought my first copy in 1949), I thought of the old Harry Temple cartoons appearing about every month in RAILROAD depicting scenes of old time railroading..Temple titled these *BACK IN THE DAYS...*Well, that seemed like a pretty good overall title for any old stuff, regardless of its origin...so, my piece became *BACK IN THE DAYS* and that's still what it's called.

When I sit down to write each month I never know exactly what's going to come out. A news item will trigger a memory, or perhaps a spate of bad winter weather will spark a thought of something that happened during my Rock Island Trainmaster days...You just can't tell...Sometimes it's Rock Island...sometime it's Burlington and sometimes it's Rock Port, Langdon and Northern. Other times, a query might come over the RITS (Rock Island Technical Society) List on the internet. For example a couple of years ago, someone wondered about the operation of trains in and out of Chicago...I posted a few of my memories in that regard...Someone asked about Piggy Back Operations on the Rock Island and I did a piece on that.

As the 2002 RITS Annual Meeting in Des Moines approached, I volunteered to do a little presentation on Chicago Operations in the 1960's..In preparation for that, I went through all my old stuff and prepared a little "handout" for my Clinic. It was only about one half of what I had gathered up...Even a good thing can be overdone...After I got the stuff gathered up that I wanted to use, I "cast about" for a title..Since most of the stories and memories related to my days as a Trainmaster on the Chicago Terminal Division, what could be better than *TERMINAL TALES.* I affixed that title to my handout, expanded it and "now you have it".

You will note that a couple of the items were contributed by my friend and colleague, Doug Weitzman...Doug followed me as night trainmaster at Blue Island when I escaped from George and the Chicago Division to the Freight Claims Department in April 1964. He later became a Division Superintendent and, after the Rock Island's demise, went on to a management position with the TRRA (Terminal Railroad Association) at St. Louis. Doug is now retired and lives in Louisville, KY.

After the Des Moines meeting, John Nelson told me that he would be interested in publishing what I had done...I gave him the stuff, and now,.. Here it is.

The items are in no particular order, and there is lots of "rambling around" from my earliest days right up through the last days of my Rock Island Experience...These are just "memory snapshots" of some of the experiences that I then "Endured with Hardship...but now..."Remember with Delight".

Maybe a little glimpse into railroading as it was, pre-computer, immediately post steam, and under the auspices of the old style Classic Military Railroad Management will give you a bit of insight as to "whence we came" and how it was "back in the days"..Hopefully you will be entertained as well as enlightened.

J. Pete Hedgpeth

ASSISTANT TO THE TRAINMASTER, ROCK ISLAND DIVISION: A HINT OF THINGS TO COME!

Chicago - November 17, 1960
File Hedgpeth, J. P.

Mr. J. B. Buffalo:

This will confirm yesterday's telephone message with you when it was decided that Operations Assistant J. P. Hedgpeth will be available for your use on the Rock Island Division as an Assistant to the Trainmaster between completion of his regular training program November 30 and January 15, 1961. This period will, of course, include the two week period at Christmas time expediting mail at Rock Island.

G. T. Gilluly

cc: J. P Hedgpeth

Rock Island - November 29,1960
File: 911-7

Mr. J. P. Hedgpeth, Operations Asst.

c/o Mr. C. U. Kitzmiller - Rock Island

As per our conversation arrange to report to:
Mr. A. Konovalski, Monday, December 5, for a two day assignment, after which return to the Tri-Cities, reporting to Mr. O. E. Morgan for assignment in connection with handling of Christmas mail.

cc: Messrs. A. Konovalski, O. E. Morgan

It's always nice to write about something as you remember it and then have an independent "third party" come back and verify what has been said. In the interest of the reputation of this piece for truth and accuracy I submit the following.

On the RITS (Rock Island Technical Society) list a few days before a recent Christmas, there had been a spate of "Christmas on the Rock Island Stories".......of course I couldn't resist saying something and here's what I wrote:

Christmas 1960.......I was an "Operations Assistant"....(Trainee) just finishing up my 12 months "training", assigned to the Rock Island Division.

It was standard practice at that time to send out the Trainees complete with Hat, Flashlight, Notebook and, for those who indulged, Cigar, to expedite the Christmas mail and passenger traffic at the major terminals. It was our job to stand around as the mail and other head end traffic was loaded...not that we could do anything to speed things up, and join the "steam chasers" after the train was made up. In case you don't know or remember what a Steam Chaser is (was). That's the official who stands at the head end of the train after it's put back together and the steam and air connections are made and "follows" the steam from the head end of the train to the rear end as it makes its way through the train. It was most satisfying to stand at the rear end and hear the promising gurgle of air, hot water and steam approaching the open steam line valve on the rear of the train. There was first a belch of hot water, then several intermittent blasts of steam, followed by more air and water until the line was clear and the steam at train line pressure reached the rear end and the car inspector gradually closed the valve until the proper feather was arranged and there was assurance that there was steam through the train and a reasonable assurance that departure was nigh.

Anyhow...it was a very cold late December or early January morning and I was on the platform at Rock Island when Number 40 arrived. It was the practice at that time to use the 2700 series Suburban Cars for mainline duty during the holiday season. Normally they didn't go beyond Rock Island but, occasionally, they went as far as Des Moines or Omaha, and apparently, this time, anyway to Kansas City.

Those of you who know this equipment know that it didn't "trainline" to other passenger equipment and had other idiosyncrasies i.e. the sliding doors would freeze and would not open. Number 40 had one of these beasts as its sole coach that morning and all of the 4 sets of sliding doors were frozen and could not be opened.

This condition presented somewhat of a problem since these cars didn't have vestibules and train No. 40 was not carrying another coach or sleeper through which the departing passengers could be herded. The conductor and his brakeman solved the exit problem by opening the end door of the car and jumping to the ground. This was not an option for the paying passengers.

What to do?? What to do??? What to do!! Your ever alert and resourceful Operations Assistant came up with the answer....The Shop Train....Said Shop Train at that time consisted of three ancient heavyweight coaches heated by coal burning stoves. Said train was stored at the passenger yard across from the depot at Rock Island. It left each morning (Mon-Fri) and went west to some point beyond Missouri Division Jct. and then came back east stopping at various points to pick up shop employees for Silvis. Fortunately this train had not yet left or perhaps it was a Saturday or Sunday morning... exactness has faded into the mists of time.

Said trainee got a hold of the conductor on the shop train

Rock Island 2700-Class Commuter Coach and the infamous "sticking doors."

and told him to cut off one coach and come against the rear of No. 40. This was done and with only minimal delay said coach was coupled to the rear of number 40's recalcitrant Suburban coach and passengers had merely to proceed through the end of said coach onto the vestibule of said shop train coach, down the steps and "viola".. The job was done.

Said Trainee received no Christmas or other bonus, nor was any official commendation placed on his record. I had forgotten about the incident when one day in the late 1970's I was visiting with one of the guys in the engineering dept. and, in what context I don't recall, he brought up the matter of the frozen doors and the shop train coach.

He was riding No. 40 that morning and, while not benefiting directly since he was going on to Chicago he did observe the move and remembered it well enough to tell me about it about 15 years later.

A couple of days after the posting on the RITS list the following appeared in my email:

Dear Mr. Hedgpeth:

"Enjoyed your story on the RITS List of number 40 and frozen doors on the 2700 series coach on the train that day. As a commuter on the Rock from the late 50's through 1964 (and occasionally thereafter), I remember the 2700s and their "freezing doors". Commuters had to be sharp because if one car's doors were frozen at a particular stop, they had to beat a hasty retreat to the next car (and an open door) before the train left that short station stop. I seem to recall that the RI trainmen kept an eye out for this to make sure that passengers had time to make the next car (not always easy with a packed/standing room only train) when they spotted a car whose doors did not open."

Signed Les Beckman (Hoosier Valley Railroad Museum/North Judson Indiana.

Seeeeee as Dave Barry would say..."I am not making this up."

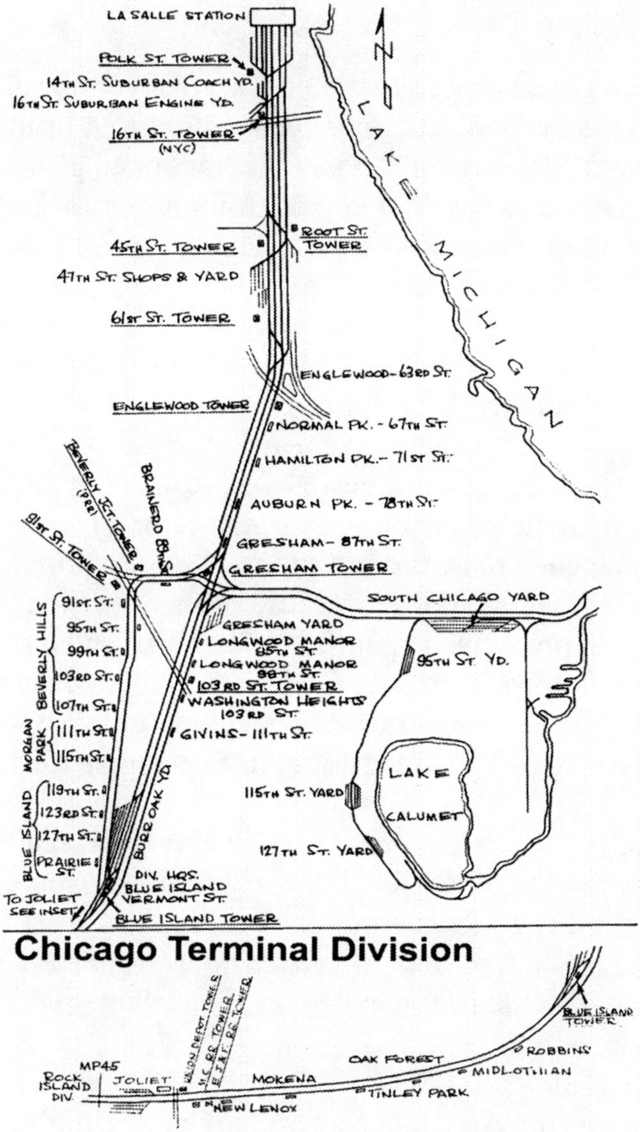

Chicago Terminal Division

ON TO THE CHICAGO DIVISION

We begin with my new orders: "J. P. Hedgpeth is assigned as Assistant Trainmaster, Chicago Division with headquarters at Joliet".

There had recently been assigned a second yardmaster at Joliet. Previously there had only been a night YM from 10:30 pm to 6:30 am. The Agent at Joliet, an appointed position (non-union) acted as day YM and the trainmaster took care of things when the agent wasn't around and supervised the yard operation in the afternoon.

Cliff Brogden, the assistant TM ahead of me had "stirred up a hornets nest" among the employees at Joliet when he discovered some drinking among a switch crew and a car inspector. The subsequent investigation resulted in the firing of a couple of switchmen and the car inspector. The car inspector happened to be the son of the Local Chairman for the SUNA (switchman's union). Because of this situation everybody had pretty well "ganged up on Cliff, and had staged a kind of "slowdown". It had gotten to the point where Cliff just couldn't get any cooperation so he chose to leave the Rock Island. That's what I found at Joliet in September 1961.

This was the first assignment I had where I was really on my own. All of the others had been in a terminal where there were always other officers around, but at Joliet at least I was 40 miles from La Salle St. Station and 25 miles from Division Headquarters at Blue Island and G. H. Voss, Superintendent.

Oliver R. Thurston (ORT) – (Tom Nebelsick will recognize the initials, was the Assistant Superintendent.) Ollie's father was one of the founders of the Order of Railroad Telegraphers and hence Oliver's name to give him the requisite initials. Oliver was a former telegrapher himself, and knew nothing about yard or terminal operations, other than in his own mind. Ollie, took me to Joliet, introduced me to Joe Jackson, the Agent and some of the other employees, took me around the facilities, told me that I had "better get the place straightened out", and as was his custom, promptly disappeared. I was on my own.

"ORT," Oliver R. Thurston who introduced me to the Rock Island's "plush" Joliet yard office had the same initials as The Order of Railroad Telegraphers which his father founded in Cedar Rapids, Iowa.

Joliet Yard met all of the standards for a Rock Island facility. Old, outmoded, too small, and worn out...totally inadequate for a modern day operation. The yard office and switchman's "shanty" were the worst I ever encountered anywhere on the system. The yard office was an ancient shack of a building, built without foundation with a wooden floor which would never allow water to stand anywhere on its surface. It slanted in every possible direction. The walls of the building leaned in all possible directions. I wish I had a picture. It was a sight to behold. The switchman's shanty was an old wooden coach sitting on the ground just east of the yard office. It was all you would expect it to be. The two buildings stood right on the edge of a foul smelling drainage ditch just below a cemetery. Wonderful surroundings.

Telephones for communication with Dispatcher or Block Operator are located as follows:

MP 15-48	MP 20-13	MP 34-6	MP 37-47	MP 43-18
MP 16-11	MP 23-17	MP 35-17	MP 41-06	MP 43-26
MP 16-36	MP 23-50	MP 35-27	MP 41-30	MP 43-33
MP 16-44	MP 28-44	MP 36-11	MP 42-00	
MP 18-16	MP 30-35	MP 37-6	MP 42-15	

Office Hours

Blue Island	Continuous	
Midlothian	7:00 A.M. to 4:00 P.M.	Daily Except Saturdays Sundays and Holiday
Oak Forest	7:00 A.M. to 4:00 P.M.	Daily Except Saturdays Sundays and Holiday
Tinley Park	7:00 A.M. to 4:00 P.M.	Daily Except Saturdays Sundays and Holiday
Mokena	6:30 A.M. to 3:30 P.M.	Daily Except Saturdays Sundays and Holiday
New Lenox	6:30 A.M. to 3:30 P.M.	Daily Except Saturdays Sundays and Holiday
Joliet	7:30 A.M. to 4:30 P.M.	Daily Except Saturdays Sundays and Holiday

O. R. THURSTON, Ass't. Supt.
R. W. PARKER, Trainmaster
F. G. VESTAL, Trainmaster
E. E. SEAL, Ass't. Trainmaster
J. E. BERGSTROM, Master Mechanic
L. C. LONNEGREN, Road Foreman Equipment
E. A. DECKER, Road Foreman Equipment
N. P. SIMON, Tower Supervisor Ass't to Trainmaster
} **Blue Island, Ill.**

J. P. HEDGPETH, Assistant Trainmaster } **Joliet, Ill.**

M. R. EWING, Chief Dispatcher
D. M. MARTIN, Assistant Chief Dispatcher
C. J. YORK, Assistant Chief Dispatcher
C. R. GIBSON, Assistant Chief Dispatcher
} **Rock Island, Ill.**

H. C. McENTIRE,
H. F. FURMAN,
A. R. MEYERS,
G. W. OLSON,
G. L. WATTS,
R. C. FEE,
K. D. HORNBAKER,
W. W. WEST,
G. R. WILLIAMSON,
C. J. STOFFER,
D. L. KIRKPATRICK,
D. N. IRWIN,
} **Dispatchers, Rock Island.**

Chicago Division 18

Chicago, Rock Island & Pacific Railroad

Rock Island

TIME TABLE

CHICAGO DIVISION

FIRST DISTRICT

No. 6

EFFECTIVE AT 12:01 A. M.
CENTRAL STANDARD TIME

SUNDAY, OCTOBER 29, 1961

G. H. VOSS,
Superintendent

B. F. WELLS, General Manager
R. H. ANDERSON, Ass't. General Manager

This Time Table for the exclusive use and guidance of Employes

The yard itself ran east and west on the north side of the double track mainline. There was a considerable grade from east to west and there was often a crisis when a car would get away, go down the lead and derail at the "J" (EJ&E) diamond. The first four tracks north of the mainlines were "through" tracks with a "wiggle" (crossovers) in the middle of the yard, right in front of the yard office. The crossovers divided the tracks 1,2,3 and 4 "above", from 1,2,3 and 4 below. The classification tracks were on the east end of the yard and were numbered 5-12. The lower lead from these tracks came back into a long lead on the north side that ran past the yard office and downgrade to the EJ&E crossing about a quarter mile to the west. The whole thing was extremely rickety and the heaviest rail was 85 lb. and most of it was lighter. The tie condition was poor to say the least and when a rail would break, Ben Long, the section foreman who was deaf as a post when he wanted to be, and never heard the phone at night when you needed him, and his gang would just get out the torch or drill and put a set of angle bars on and that was the repair.

The Rock Island had lots of industries in the Joliet area. Most of them were "west of the river". The river was the Illinois Ship Canal which hosted lots of industries which were constantly polluting the water. The river flowed through the middle of Joliet and divided the city into the east side and west side. There were about 5 or 6 drawbridges which crossed the river to accommodate automobile traffic and one over which the Rock Island ran. More bridge stories later.

Lots of traffic for the Rock Island was generated by Caterpillar, Amoco Chemical, Freeport Sulfur, Illinois River Terminal, Rockdale Industrial District, and a couple of paper companies. There were numerous small industries

Jet Rocket in commuter service at "my" station where, later on, I commuted to and from LaSalle Street Station.

scattered around what was known as the "lower yard" which at one time had been the main yard and on the mainline, before the mainline had been relocated years ago when the river had been channelized.

So much for the layout. Here was the operation. First trick: 2 engines starting at the yard office. A 6:30 am yard job which switched the classification yard and did an industry or two a 7:59 am West of the River Job which got his cars together and went west to switch Caterpillar and some of the other industries. Second trick: A 2:30 pm yard job, a 3:00 pm west of the river job which did the industries immediately west of the river and a 3:59 pm west of the river job which did the industries far out on the Amoco lead track. Third trick: a 10:30 pm yard job and a 11:00 pm coach job, which went to the Joliet UD and lined up the suburban coaches for the morning trains.

There were about 6 trains which originated at Joliet each morning, one of which was comprised of the infamous Aerotrain or Jet Rocket. Those of you old enough to remember will recall that in the mid-1950's there was a push to adopt a new light weight rail technology to long distance rail travel. I recall that the Jet Rocket was the TALGO TRAIN or TRAIN X developed by ACF. The Aerotrain was developed by GM.

After these trains had worn out their welcome on the NYC and some other railroads, the RI in it's usual less than astute purchasing policy picked up two of the Aerotrains -- after all the Jet Rocket was already in service. It was John Farrington's hope that the Jet Rockets would provide high speed mainline service even so far as thinking that the Jet Rocket was appropriate for the Rocky Mountain Rocket, but the Jet Rocket had problems not to mention the newly acquired Aerotrains. What a disaster....We'll talk more about episodes with these museum pieces later.

The coach yard at Joliet was located near the depot, about a mile or so west of the yard. It consisted of two storage tracks south of the two main tracks on "the elevation" west of the depot and a couple of tracks "in the hole" on the north side. These tracks ran from the elevated main line down to street level to serve the freight depot and Joliet Packing, a wholesale meat operation. The 1949 vintage air conditioned double door cars were stored on these lower tracks and the old 2500 series coaches (the ones you see now on most tourist railroads) were stored up above on the elevation along with the Aerotrain or Jet Rocket.

Each night the switch engine had to go down and make the necessary cuts and rearrange the coaches for the suburban trains. It shouldn't have been a big job, but the crews made it an all night affair in most cases. More about that later.

Now that you have a very rough idea of what Joliet was like in terms of operation and layout, I'll just relate a few incidents which occurred while I was there without regard for chronology.

THE ED DICKENS EPISODE

In late September or Early October, one of the switchmen came in the office one afternoon to inform me that I had better look out and prepare for trouble, because Ed Dickens had just been put back to work after being fired for a year for fighting with a switchman. I was told that Ed was a notorious troublemaker and that there was a rough road ahead. OK so what else is new? They told me that Ed had bid in the 2:30 pm yard engine and that he would be on the job the next Sunday afternoon.

JOSEPH VAN GAMPLER
YARDMASTER
JOLIET

On the railroad in those pre-enlightened management days, Sunday was no different than any other day for Trainmasters, and I had to be there to oversee things. We did have a yardmaster on Sunday mornings, so I usually checked in with him, before church, then afterwards had lunch at home and came down about 1:00 pm. After I got there, I usually let Joe Van Gampler, the YM go home early since there was nothing going on.

On this day, knowing about "the return of Ed Dickens", Joe wished me success with Ed and went on his way.

About 1:15 or so, I was sitting in the *plush* yardmaster and trainmaster's quarters alone when a car drove up into the parking area. It was a warm fall afternoon so I walked out to see who it was. A man got out and walked into the yard office and back to where I was standing. He introduced himself as Ed Dickens and asked if he could come in and talk to me alone. I invited him into my "office" and closed the door.

Ed said something to the effect that he supposed that I had heard that he was coming down and that I knew something of his reputation and most recent difficulty. I replied that I did.

Ed said to me with great sincerity... I have learned my lesson, I've turned over a new leaf, and I don't ever want anything like what I've been through to happen to me again. I just want you to know that I'll cooperate with you in anything you want me to do. Just tell me what you want and I'll do it, I don't care what it is. I assured him that I appreciated his coming in and that his past indiscretions would not play a part in anything that happened from now on. He thanked me and again told me over and over that he was so glad to be back to work and that he was going to be, in effect, Mr. Congeniality. I assured him that I did appreciate it and would act accordingly.

Ed proved to be as good as, if not better than, his word. Every day, he would come in early to talk to me and ask how he was doing, and if there was anything he could do for me. He would occasionally come in and report to me, after swearing me not to divulge him as the source, when the crew was dogging it or other violations. Ed even taught me a little bit about running an engine and using the automatic air. Whenever I would go out to ride with his crew, he would always ask me if I wanted to run the engine. He was the most changed man, based on his former reputation that I have ever seen.

Later, long after I had left Joliet and even left the operating department, I would be occasionally riding the suburban train Ed was running. Whenever he would see me on the platform he would always lean out and yell and wave at me. During my last years at the Rock Island Ed was pulling *The Banker's Special* from Joliet and he took to wearing a suit, because in his words, "If I'm going to pull all those big shots, I better be dressed up". Ed is probably long retired and perhaps even passed on by now. He was probably in his mid 50's when I was at Joliet in 1961 and 62.

Rather than be completely chronological I'll just relate some of the more significant events that occurred during my tenure at Joliet, giving an appropriate title to each one. Here they are for your amusement, edification, or boredom as the case may be.

WORKING OUT PROBLEMS IN TRANSPORTATION PART 1: HOT CAR

During my time in the Management Training Program, I had gotten acquainted with and became quite good friends with a fellow "Trainee", Earl Seal. Earl was a bit older than I and was from Mississippi. He had worked for the GM&O as a yard clerk, and had a world of stories of his own regarding such characters as B.C. and Pearly. . Earl was tall, sandy haired and always smoked a pipe. He spoke with a Mississippi drawl and never got excited.

Earl had finished the training program before me and had been assigned as night trainmaster at Blue Island. A really hot and disagreeable job I later inherited for about two years.

Earl and George Voss never hit it off. George couldn't relate to anyone with a slow southern mentality or method of operating. Consequently he was always after Earl about something and seemed to take particular delight in tormenting him continually. With all of the things that could go wrong in a large terminal operation such as Blue Island, it wasn't hard for George to find things to criticize and he did. Ultimately Earl couldn't abide the situation any longer and left the Rock Island.

Anyhow....Each night it was the practice, if sufficient cars warranted it, to operate a Blue Island - Silvis local known as THE RED BALL PICKUP. Originally the theory had been that this train would leave BI shortly after midnight with the "short" cars, pick up the hot loads between Joliet and Silvis and get to the Silvis terminal in time to go over the hump ahead of No.'s 81 and 91, the Denver and California Hotshots. As with most railroad theories in that day, it never worked that way. The RBPU seldom got out of BI before 5:00 am. (There's a classic story about that too for later). And seldom got to Silvis before noon or later. It was just a plain old mainline local with sometimes 80-100 cars.

Every night the Blue Island Trainmaster (Earl), the Joliet Trainmaster (me) and the Chief Dispatcher at Rock Island would confer to see if we had, 1. Sufficient cars to warrant a train; 2. Available power; 3. A rested crew. Usually the train was operated at least Sunday night through Thursday night, and occasionally on the weekends. If there were only a few cars or no power the train just wasn't operated.

On a particular night in late '61 or early '62 Earl called with his usual query as to whether I had any short cars for the west. We had none that night. Earl said that he had only a very few, certainly not enough for a train, but there was a problem.

In the Blue Island Yard sat a car of meat which had come in from the east destined for Joliet Packing. This car, of course, had to be moved to Joliet and spotted first thing the next morning. Normally Earl would have just put the car on the head end of the RBPU, it would have been set out at Joliet and we would have spotted it at Joliet Packing after the suburban trains left in the morning.

Comes the "rub". Do you run a train for one car of perishable or do you delay the car. We were between the proverbial rock and hard place. Earl didn't want to rout George out to ask him. The Chief Dispatcher didn't want to make a decision... Earl said, "I've got an idea, I'll call you back in a little while. The time would have been about 9:00 to 10:00 pm.

Earl called back in awhile with this scheme. No. 59 THE PBX (Piggy Back Express) was the hottest train on the railroad. He was due out of Blue Island at 2:00 am and into Denver the next morning at 4:30. At that time the railroad was still in good enough physical condition that it usually worked. Only piggybacks and tri-levels of automobiles and sometimes some auto parts were to move on this train. Any delay brought repercussions from the top. Get the picture. This was a HOT TRAIN, not to be delayed for anything.

Earl said in his slow Mississippi drawl, "Jeeeem, (I was Jim in those days), what do you think about this...What if we call 59 about 30 minutes early and try to get him out at least 15 minutes ahead of time (that would be 1:45 am, instead of 2:00). I'm going to put the car of meat behind the caboose out of Blue Island and see if the crew will take it that way. If they balk I'll tell them that I'm going to put it on the head end and they'll have to stop at Joliet and set it out."

If I can get them to do it, can you have a switch engine at the "middle connection" (a crossover from track No. 1 to the north main track used for pickups and setouts) and grab the car off the mainline. I told him that I thought that was a great idea, and that I would stay down at the yard to be sure that all went as planned. We wondered together whether we should call George and ask him, but decided not to. If anything went wrong we probably would both be fired, but I was young (25) and game.

The time went by....Earl had the train called for 1:15 instead of the usual 1:45. This put the crew on duty at 12:45 (30 minutes prep time). Earl had said earlier, I hope it's a cooperative conductor, and not one of the other kind that were in the majority at that time. Wouldn't you know it was one of the crabby ones... I don't remember which one.

About 1:30, after he had gone over to the yard office and told the conductor what he was going to do, Earl called and said that finally after a lot bitching and talk of "it being against the rules to send a train out of the yard with a car behind the caboose etc, etc, etc" and his finally telling the crew that they take it on the rear end or he would put it on the head end and they would have to set it out. This was an idle threat because we had decided that this would cost too much delay and we couldn't cover it up and keep it off the delay report, but the crew didn't know this.

It was agreed that the meat with a red lantern (A 1961 "FRED") affixed to the rear coupler would go behind the caboose of NO. 59 out of Blue Island. It was also agreed that 59 would stop at the middle connection at Joliet, cut off the car and go. There would be a switch engine waiting to take the car off the mainline.

All was in readiness. Fortunately the trailers were tied down at Blue Island and 12th St. in decent time and Earl got 59 out about 1:45 am. When that was accomplished, he called me and advised that all had gone OK on his end.

In the meantime, I had stayed to line up Ned Barnett, the night yardmaster as to what we were going to do, and that no matter what else was going on, that switch engine had to be at the middle connection when 59 stopped. It was about a 25 minute run for 59 from Blue Island to Joliet yard.

2:10 am: The Joliet yard engine is standing at the middle connection. J. Pete Hedgpeth and YM Ned Barnett are standing by the radio in the yard office. Comes the call...."No. 59 callin' the Joliet Yard. Joliet Yard....59's got this car of meat for you behind the caboose. What do we do?"

Ned said "you just pull the rear end over the middle connection, turn the angle cock, pull the pin and go."

"Well, is that switch engine, gonna be there, we're not leavin no car on the mainline unless that engine's there to take it...."

Time for "management" to get in the act. TM Hedgpeth... "This is the trainmaster speaking, we'll be right there to take the car and responsibility for it. You just cut it off, give the bill to the engine foreman and get out of town. Don't worry about the lantern, we'll take care of that too."

"OK...."

No. 59 made a perfect stop just over the connection. I went over to get the bill. 59 left town -- and probably hadn't stopped more than 30 seconds. The switch engine went out, got the car and brought it down to the yard office. The deed was done. Now for the COVER UP…

The Chief Dispatcher knew what we were doing, but I can't remember what we agreed to show as delay at Joliet, maybe stopped at the E&JE or C&A (GM&O) crossings. Since 59 was ahead of time, we may have committed the PERFECT CRIME and gotten away with it. I just don't remember what the dispatcher did.

There was another consideration now for Earl and me....Do we tell George what we did? After 59 was on his way, I called Earl to report, he of course was listening on the radio and the tower line intercom so he knew what was happening.

We discussed the pros and cons as to whether we should "confess" to George. We decided that Earl had better tell him, since the punishment would probably be worse if he didn't tell him and George found out on his own. It was almost impossible to keep anything from George. Earl decided to make a full disclosure of the dastardly deed when George came in at 6:30 am.

The next evening when Earl came to work about 6:00 pm he called me as we had agreed, to tell me George's reaction. Earl told me that he gave George all the details as to what had been done, and why, and how he had arranged the 'cover up'. George's response.... "Well don't think you can do that every night".

This was a characteristic response from an operating officer of the old school. Never a word of praise for using a bit of creativity or initiative. If anything went wrong "they'd want to fire you".

It was a different world at that time, but things had begun to change.

WORKING OUT PROBLEMS IN TRANSPORTATION
Part 2: PEDALING THE SHORTS

In the last section, I had occasion to refer to a train known as THE REDBALL PICKUP. I explained a bit about its function and alleged purpose, but later I got to thinking that probably no one but us old guys know the origin of the term "redball". This is my understanding of how the term came to be used.

Years ago, before the days of the computer, or even the teletype machine, which was the ultimate in technology during my active railroading days, there was only one way to know the contents of a carload of goods. That means was just to look at the waybill, which is nothing more than a document that authorizes the movement of a car, either loaded or empty. The waybill is prepared by the railroad which originates the shipment, it specifies the car number, originating carrier, routing (which railroad is to take the car where), contents, weight and other information necessary to get the shipment where it is going.

Obviously some shipments have a higher priority than others and hence need to be expedited in preference to other shipments when, as quite often occurs, everything in the yard cannot be moved on the first or fastest train. Consequently something was needed to inform such functionaries as yardmasters and conductors as to the relative importance of carload shipments.

Some carrier, back in the dim and distant past hit upon the idea of placing a red circular sticker on the upper right hand corner of the waybill to indicate a priority load, to be given preference over other shipments and to be expedited off the "rip" tracks and other places of potential delay. Hence the term 'REDBALL' came to mean a priority shipment or by extension a train to be expedited and not subject to delay. Hence a REDBALL train was a train to be expedited. An additional designation on the Rock Island was GOLDBALL. GOLDBALL indicated a priority shipment for California i.e. auto parts, merchandise etc. It was even of a higher priority than REDBALL which was used to designate shipments from Chicago to Denver or perhaps the pacific northwest via St. Paul, Minneapolis. Now don't you feel that your life is more complete since you have that information.

Anyhow, the REDBALL PICKUP (RBPU) was supposed to

leave Burr Oak Yard at Blue Island each night right after the PBX (Piggyback Express), set out cars at Joliet and other stations "short" of Silvis and pick up cars (supposedly REDBALL) for Silvis and west.

Union agreements for train and enginemen required, probably still do, that "shorts" in a local are to be lined up in "station order" from the head end of the train, i.e. cars for the station closest to the terminal originating the train would be next to the engine, the next station behind those etc. The idea being that the crew making the setout would always have the cars to be set out next to the engine. The complication begins when you have a train making setouts or pickup at intermediate stations. Additional complications arise when those intermediate stations have their own yards and switching districts handled by switch engines. There is no problem with a local making two or more setouts or pickups or doing switching at a station where no yard engine is employed. However where there are yard engines employed more than one setout or pickup by a road train is considered switching and therefore both the road crew and switch crew can file a time claim for additional pay (usually an additional day's pay) for making more than one setout or pickup at an intermediate station where yard engines work.

The Chicago and the part of the Illinois Division, Joliet to Silvis (QUAD CITIES) comprised the heaviest concentration of industry on the Rock Island System. There were those who referred to the area along the Illinois River from Joliet to just east of Bureau Jct. as the Ruhr Valley of the United States, or at least of the Rock Island.

Here's how the stations line up from Blue Island west to Silvis, I'll indicate with an S stations that are served by a switch engine. Blue Island, Midlothian, Oak Forrest, Tinley Park, Mokena, New Lenox, Joliet (S), Minooka, Morris (S), Seneca (S), Marseilles (S), Ottawa (S), La Salle-Peru (S),

Spring Valley, Depue (S), Bureau, Annawan, Atkinson, Geneseo and Silvis.

The communities between Blue Island and Joliet were predominately residential, although there was a team track off the south track switch on east end at Oak Forrest, an elevator track on the north side off the north track at Tinley Park, switch on both ends, a track on each side switches on both ends at Mokena, and a short elevator track on the south side, off the south track, switch on east end at New Lenox.

The problem of getting the few industries between Joliet and Blue Island taken care of was the responsibility of the Joliet Trainmaster as Boss Hogg used to say---- "Namely me". Although he had little say over how the trains were run. The usual practice was for the RBPU to take care of any switching at Mokena and Tinley Park on the north side. That was relatively easy. Although the territory from MP 43 west of Joliet to Blue Island was CTC and both tracks were signaled in both directions, trains were normally run on the right hand track. So westbound trains i.e. the RBPU would take care of switching the industries on the north side and eastbound trains would do the south side.

The complications were the lumber yard at Mokena on the south side and the team track at Oak Forrest on the south side. The usual lineup was for Blue Island to send cars for these industries to Joliet where they would be put on an eastbound train to be set out and spotted at the appropriate locations. Here's what usually happened. Trains 45 and 46 were Blue Island - Peoria trains which operated nightly except No 45 on Saturday night and No. 46 on Sunday night. 46 was due out of Peoria around 9-10 pm, did a bit of local work along the way, picking up Chicago cars at La Salle, Ottawa, Joliet etc. We were supposed to give 46 any short cars for the south side at New Lenox, Mokena, Tinley Park and Oak Forrest.

The usual routine when we had a car for Mokena or Oak Forrest to add to 46 at Joliet, was that 46 was usually later than he should be and his engines stood for 81 and the GSX, due out of BI at 11:00 and 12:00. Hence the chief dispatcher would tell the Joliet YM not to give 46 any short cars. Even if we had already added these short cars, the dispatcher would have MC Tower tell 46 to do no local work from Joliet to BI.

There were several periods of time where a load of lumber for the team track at Oak Forrest spent more than a week cycling between Blue Island and Joliet. It was especially exciting to get calls from the lumber yard owner stating that he had seen his car of lumber go by 3 times in the last week, and he wondered if maybe sometime we could set it out for him. I think that's what he said anyway.....Then George Voss would call and would open his conversation in the usual way "HEDGPATH....(sic), This is VOSS, 'I mean to say'" George opened all conversations this way, "How come you don't spot that lumber at Oak Forrest?" After telling him what he already knew about the dispatcher telling 46 to run the work, I would still get a tongue lashing about not getting the work done on my territory etc. He always finished up his "harangues" with the statement "How am I going to explain this to Management". Sometimes "management" usually in the person of the Vice President Traffic or the Vice President of Operations got the call direct from the customer. Then the calls from George were even more exciting "I just got a call from Mr. Limestall, or Mr. Tharp etc.. How can I explain this to them". Such was the joy of being on the Chicago Division and under the eye of "Management". Most lumber yard owners in Hallam, NE or Smith Center, Kansas wouldn't have called the VP, but in the Chicago area they did.

So much for the work between Blue Island and Joliet. Now for the operation west of Joliet. Under normal operation the RBPU would have left Blue Island with his train lined up from the head end like this. Joliet's, Morris, Seneca, Marseilles,

Ottawa, La Salle, Depue, Bureau, then the Silvis and west cars on the rear end.

If we were following the same kind of guideline at Joliet, we would have the RBPU pickup line up the same way from west to east: Morris, Seneca, Marseilles, Ottawa, La Salle, Depue, Bureau then Silvis and west.

If the RBPU had made his Joliet setout and picked up our "short" cars you can see that he would have cars for each of the above stations in two places in his train, i.e. from the head end after his Joliet pickup Morris, Seneca, Marseilles, Ottawa, Utica (I forgot to put Utica in before, there was also a switch engine there) La Salle, Depue, Bureau, Silvis and west then again Morris, Seneca, Marseilles, etc.

The situation had been going on for sometime creating complaints and "timeslips", when someone hit upon what I thought was an ingenuous solution to the problem. It required some negotiation with the operating unions, but things were ironed out and here's how we worked it.

The RBPU left BI with his Joliet cars on the head end for set out and behind them his Illinois Division shorts lined up in traditional station order i.e., from the head end, Morris, Seneca, Marseilles, Ottawa, etc. At Joliet we lined up our Illinois Division shorts in an arrangement called "Dutching". That is the order of the shorts was with the cars for the station furthest away "down first" or on the head or west end. In other words in reverse station order. Does this mean Dutchmen are backward???

When the RBPU would get to Joliet, he would cut off his train on the mainline, and pull his Joliet's into the yard. He would cut off his power and back onto our "dutched" shorts and shove back onto his train. His train would now line up with our Seneca cars coming against Seneca cars he had in his train after he made his Morris setout etc. If you want a clearer picture, draw a diagram, if you don't just forget it, you probably weren't interested anyway.

The arrangement did necessitate the RBPU hanging onto a bunch of cars in making his setouts, but it solved the problem of two setouts at the local stations.

In case you're interested in what we did with the "through" Silvis cars, we added them to the rear end with the switch engine after the RBPU pulled down.

WORKING OUT PROBLEMS IN TRANSPORTATION Part 3: A SUPEREROGATORY EFFORT!

Shortly after the turn of the year from 1961-62 the thermometer headed for the basement. There was a period of time beginning about mid January and extending for nearly a month when the weather forecast would read: "high today about –5 degrees. Nighttime lows would range from –15 to –25. Not to mention the wind chill figure which we didn't use back then!. A real fun time to be operating a fleet of decrepit suburban equipment, to say nothing of the attendant problems with the regular freight and switching operations.

As related before, Joliet was, and still is the western terminal for the Rock Island Suburban operation. At that time we had about 6 trains heated by steam plus the Jet Rocket (which had its own set of problems in good weather or bad), which terminated and were stored at the coach yard at the Joliet Union Depot. The coach yard consisted of two storage tracks "in the hole". The hole was two tracks at ground level, as opposed to the other tracks which were on the "elevation". The hole tracks were connected to the north main track just east of the Des Plaines River Bridge. The bridge was a LIFT SPAN, which could be, and frequently was, raised to allow river traffic to pass through. When the bridge was up, you couldn't pull out of the hole with a cut of cars, since the switch was only about 50 feet from the east end of the lift span. A typical Rock Island convoluted operation.

All of the steam heated trains except for one 8 car train which consisted of what we called THE AC's (the heavyweight, depressed door, air conditioned cars which the Rock Island purchased in 1949 as a first attempt at modernizing its suburban service--these also were, I believe the first air-conditioned cars on any railroad in the Chicago area). As mentioned before the AC's were numbered in the 2700 series – the cars with the "sticky doors."

All of the other trains consisted of the standard Rock Island steam heated suburban cars in the 2500 series. These are the cars you see on the tourist railroads today. They were built, I believe in 1926 and replaced the wooden, open vestibule cars previously used. They were of extremely simple construction, high off the rail and easy to work on. These cars had no provision for making electricity except for some batteries (which were of course, always dead) for so called "emergency lights". The cars were "train-lined" together through a cable connector which passed from car to car overhead through the vestibules. The cables always hung down enough to knock the hat off a tall man passing between the cars. The train-line extended to the locomotive, which were mostly the Alco road switchers, which was equipped with a generator directly connected to the crankshaft to provide electricity for the cars. These engines also were equipped with a steam generator in the nose (short end) to provide steam for heating.

As long as the cars were connected to the locomotive, and the steam generator on said locomotive continued to function, and the train wasn't too long, and the steam generator didn't run out of water, and the fireman kept the train-line pressure high enough the train would heat fairly well. You noticed a considerable number of variables, connected by "and" in the preceding sentence. A failure of any of these variables could result in disaster, i.e. a "'froze' up train".

Two other items added to the mix providing wintertime fun for Rock Island Operating Men on the Chicago Division. I bet you thought of at least one of them. How were the trains kept warm overnight when stored at Joliet? In the basement of the Joliet Freight House were two boilers, the old and the new, (remarkable creativity in naming.) The old boiler, located in a pit at the east end of the freight house basement was exactly what you would expect it to be...an old locomotive boiler. This unit leaked considerably and to say the least, it was not efficient. At the other end of the basement was a modern "package boiler" which was far more efficient and would put out about twice the volume of steam than the old boiler would produce. With no coaches on the lines you could get the boiler pressure up to about 110 lbs. which would be comparable, although somewhat less than a locomotive steam generator would produce. They would go up to 150 lbs. or more. On a cold night with all the coaches on line and both boilers going it was sometimes possible to see space between the pressure gauge needle and the 0 mark. Sometimes if you took one train off it would go up to 5 lbs. Get the picture....

To provide supplemental steam, we would bring one or two suburban engines which laid over at the Joliet Engine-house, down to the depot and connect them to one or two of the trains on the storage track. This of course, required calling out a fireman to "watch" the engine and keep the steam generators going. The water capacity of the locomotive steam generator tank wasn't much, so a couple of times each night the engines would have to be cut off and run back to the house for water. Of course while they were gone the cars would start to freeze up. They also had to be cut off and watered before taking the trains out in the morning so it was fun all night. I spent almost all night every night at the coach yard during that 30-day period. Always with suit and tie on. No operating officer was permitted to dress otherwise. Much of the time was spent crawling under the coaches with fusees and torches made with rags soaked with oil on wires trying to thaw out the steam traps and get the cars to heat.

I've alluded to the inability to pull a cut of coaches out of the hole when the bridge was up. The yardmaster would try to coordinate movements out of the hole with the bridge-tender to avoid having the coaches being switched out of the hole off steam for too long a period. He would try to coordinate with the engine foreman, who was mostly interested in overtime and staying out of the cold, and the bridge-tender, who although a railroad employee, seemingly always gave preference to river traffic. The typical scenario was the YM would call the bridge-tender and tell him the engine was ready to come out with the coaches. The bridge-tender would tell him OK. The engine would pull up the hill and you would hear on the tower line intercom "bridge goin' up"....The coaches would sit there and freeze while a barge tow maneuvered its way by....Such is how it was.

Now to the main point of the SUPEREROGATORY EFFORT.

There was one other variable in the ROCK ISLAND WINTER CARNIVAL. That was the 12th St. coach yard which jutted south of the La Salle St. Station. This is where the suburban cars were stored during the day. Guess what kind of facilities this terminal possessed to keep the coaches warm and prepared for the evening suburban trains. You only get one guess....NONE.

Here was the operating plan in cold weather. As the inbound trains would pass by the 16th St. Tower, the rear brakeman would yank the communicating whistle cord 6 times. The signal for the fireman to shut off the train heat. The trainman would then quickly open the steam valve on the train-line on the rear of the train. There would be a tremendous roar and plume of steam from the rear of the train as the line cleared itself. With the steam generator being shut off, the theory was that the line would blow itself dry, and the traps would allow the steam in the coach heating lines to condense and run back into the train line in a relatively small volume which, even if it froze, it wouldn't matter much.

The train would pull up to the post at La Salle St. and disgorge its passengers. The train crew would then beat it up the platform, turn in their tickets and cash fares, and race up La Salle St. to their jobs as messengers at the Chicago Board of Trade, or as department store clerks. A switchman pilot would board the rear of the train.. try the air, whistle three times and the road engine crew would back the train out of La Salle St., down the hill to the 12th St. Coach Yard and into a storage track. There would be a car inspector to cut the engine off, breaking the steam and air connections. Polk St. Tower would line the engine back out of the main tracks and he would head down a clear track through the 12th St. coach yard to the "engine terminal" at 16th St. Engine terminal is an exaggeration. It consisted of a couple of tracks where the suburban engines sat during the day. There was a fueling facility and a water hose to water the steam generators. That was it.

Now the event that generated the need for "SUPEREROGATORY EFFORT. One morning, some hapless trainman didn't do his job of blowing out the steam-line as his train passed 16th St. Tower. Remember this is still during the ICE AGE of 1961-1962. The train got to the coach yard with its train-line full of steam. I don't know how they got the engine cut off without someone getting scalded, but apparently it happened.

The train, with its inside the coach heating pipes, its steam traps and train-line full of water sat on the 12th St. yard all day in Zero weather. I don't know who made the discovery, but when they put the engine on the train for its evening departure it was discovered that the train-line was a solid block of ice. A solidly frozen train-line doesn't thaw easily in Zero weather so there was only one thing to do about the situation...Get the train out of town and let someone else worry about fixing it.

The train of course was a 10 car Joliet train. I don't know how I found out about it, but apparently one of the clerks at the yard had found out and told me. I hadn't had any "official" notice yet, but it wasn't long in coming. It took its usual form.

"HEDGPATH...sic,"

"Yes Sir..."

"This is Voss…"

"Yes Sir..."

"I'm (George did everything personally) sending you a 10 car train out of La Salle St. and its completely froze up".

"Yes Sir…"

"I mean it's all froze up, train-line and all."

"OK...."

"Now I want you to get that train thawed out tonight...I want it warm and I want it out of there in the morning on time."

"Yes sir, we'll do our best to take care of it."

"Did you hear me Hedgpath...I said I want that train out of there warm and on time tomorrow morning, Do you understand me...?"

"Yes Sir." What to do now...?

We were using an extra carman at the depot each night to assist the regular man, so we didn't have an abundance of mechanical department help. Joliet had a RIP track at that time and we had 3 or 4 carmen working there so I thought that we had better get all of them. I called either the Mechanical Foreman, Larry Miller, who never was much help, or Ray Zivic, the lead carman and told them what we had coming. I said you better get all the help out you can find.

I went down to the depot to meet the train which arrived about 6:00. It was of course, pretty dark by them. The passengers got off. They were of course in a delightful humor having ridden 40 miles over an hour or so in coaches which were about as cold as it was outside.

We had a switch engine bring the entire train up to the engine-house-rip track area and shove it down an unused track. I thought it would be better to be close to the mechanical facilities. Ray had rounded up a couple of his men and they were there. It was overtime stuff so they came right out. I asked Ray what he was going to do. He said, “You just watch”.

Remember, all of the inside pipes were frozen and the steam-line though the car underneath was frozen solid along with the traps, which separate out the water from the condensation in the pipes in the car.

We watered and fueled a suburban engine and coupled it to the train. Hooked up the steam line and put boiler pressure against the train line. Ray and his boys had gathered up a number of 5 gallon open top cans. They sat two of the cans in the aisle of each car each about 1/3 of the way down. They then poured about 2-3 inches of alcohol into these cans and set it ablaze. They had built two campfires in each coach. The idea was that we had to warm the interior of the cars to get the inside pipes thawed to allow the steam to come through.

They then went outside, starting with the head car, and began to thaw the train-lines with their homemade torches. As the steam from the engine combined with the thawing of the torches outside began to let the steam through the train-line, the traps began to break open and as the interior of the car warmed up the inside pipes thawed and let some steam in. It was a long process...They worked all night, but finally got the train thawed out in the early morning hours.

Rock Island 2500-class commuter coach at the Boone and Scenic Valley Railroad, Boone, Iowa

Assistant Trainmaster's view of the same car.

We hustled the train back down to the depot with the engine still on. It was ready for departure, on time and warm. They got the entire train thawed out except for one side of one car.

The train did indeed depart on time and warm, however the interior conditions were not all that could be desired by an exacting traveler. The burning alcohol had created a bit of soot and the interior of the coaches, including the windows were covered with a greasy black film, but we had done our job. The train was out on time and it was warm.

I commended the rip track boys on a good job, and they were also thanked in their paychecks the next half.

I'm still waiting for my commendation from George, who has since passed away or from "management" most of whom are long gone too.

WHAT'S IN A NAME? Part 1

From 2:30 pm until about 4:30 pm Monday - Friday were the busiest time at the Joliet Yard. As previously mentioned we had round-the-clock yard engines, then a 3:00 pm industry job and a 3:59 pm industry job which went west over the Illinois River and worked the industries on what was called the AMOCO SPUR.

The Conductor on the 3:00 pm industry job was Ed Seeley. Ed was an extremely witty fellow and a real "high class guy". He was about 6'3" and weighed in at 225 or more. With his gray hair and neat appearance he could have passed for an executive of a major corporation. Ed's engineer was quite the opposite. His name was Ed Ledebuhr. An old German, I guess, about 60 years old or more. Ed always wore dirty old striped overalls and chewed tobacco evidence of which always ran from the corners of his mouth. Ed was not what you would call "an artist" with the automatic air. His crew constantly complained about how he roughed them up in the caboose. He was content to complete his years to retirement working an afternoon switch engine, and apparently had no desire to work the mainline. Ed was a real "kidder" and tormentor of other employees, although not with the wit and sophistication of Ed Seeley. Ed's main source of pleasure and amusement was antagonizing the engineer on the 3:59 pm industry job. That worthy's name was Ira W. Hobby.

"Hobby" was what he wanted to be called. When introduced and his new acquaintance would refer to him as "Ira". He always said "just call me Hobby". His middle name was to this time unknown by anyone and is the source of this little reminiscence.

Hobby's conductor was Dick Doolin. Dick hailed from Trenton, MO and was a first class switchman. He and his crew liked their overtime, and got from 4 to 6 hours each night, but they got the work done. Hobby's skill with the brake valve was similar to Ledebuhr's. Doolin wasn't a complainer, but once in a while, he would comment that "Damn... Hobby's awful rough sometimes". Hobby was probably, like Ledebuhr about 60 years old, quite heavy and bald headed with some of his teeth out. Again a typical switch engine engineer working out his years to retirement. Hobby was a good natured kind of guy with a loud voice. He was quite a talker, but not the wit or tormentor that Ledebuhr or Seeley were.

For many years it had been a long-term project of Hobby's fellow employees to find out what his middle initial stood for. Hobby stubbornly refused to reveal anything.

On this memorable afternoon. The yard engine, having gone to work at 2:30 was at the "top end' of the yard making up the two industry job's trains and sorting out the yard. Seeley's crew was lounging in the yard office waiting for their 3:00 pm start time. Ed was always there early to get his work lineup and visit with the clerks and switchmen. As afternoon "Yardmaster" it was my job to line up the work for the engines and get them started. Ed had come in and I had given him his work lineup and told him the "J's" (interchange for the EJ&E") were on track 2 below, and that as usual, the J delivery would be his first job. Ed went out to get his crew started and then came back in to "jaw" with the others. At this time of day there were always 5-10 men in and out of the plush yard office. The day YM, Joe Van Gampler was usually still around, the day clerk, Nick Green, would be giving his "turnover" to the afternoon clerk, Bob Brown or Bob Meyesmberg, and Joe Carigan, the operator was on duty until 4:00 pm. Since there were three switch crews going to work there could be 6-8 switchmen standing around also.

Hobby always came down to work early. Although his job didn't go to work until 3:59 pm he was always there about 3:00 or shortly thereafter. As usual Seeley began to needle Hobby about his middle name and Hobby as was his custom refused any information. I don't know what Seeley finally said, I wasn't physically present when the revelation came, but Hobby, upon a promise of total secrecy from Seeley not to reveal it to another living soul confessed to Seeley that his name was none other than WINFIELD.

Hobby then went out to get his engine and go to work. Of course Seeley's promise of "secrecy" lasted about 5 minutes. Just long enough for Hobby to get outside. Ed Seeley couldn't wait to get out and report the findings to Ed Ledebuhr, Hobby's chief tormentor.

All was well for a few minutes. Seeley's crew and Doolin's crew were busy back and forth and in and out of several yard tracks making up their cuts. I happened to look out of the window, just as Ledebuhr's engine passed Hobby's engine on the lead track. Just as the engine windows passed each other, over the radio came, without benefit of any introduction

Ledebuhr's voice at full volume saying... ***"WHATDOYA SAY THERE... WINFIELD OLD BOY...."***

Hobby's secret was out and broadcast for all the world to hear. He should have known that Seeley would lose no time in disseminating the news and he didn't. From then on HOBBY WAS OUT...WINFIELD WAS IN...

I also earned a nickname while Trainmastering at Joliet.

WHAT'S IN A NAME? Part 2

You will recall the story of Ed Dickens, the reformed "fighter" who indeed turned over a new leaf recounted earlier? There was another engineer with a reputation for trouble making who didn't.

Floyd Hall was a man about 60 or more, who had a reputation for drinking and extremely obnoxious, surly and insubordinate behavior. He had been barred from main-line service and was restricted to a switch engine. He lived in Joliet, so consequently he "bumped" on the afternoon yard engine one day during the winter of 1961-62. All of the switchmen "hated his guts". He was very hardnosed and wouldn't let the switchmen do things they usually did. An example: It was the habit of the switchmen to remove "dunnage" (wood blocks, braces etc) from cars in the yard and load the stuff on the engine and bring the stuff down to the yard office or pile it up to burn for a fire during cold weather.

Well when Floyd came on the job he wouldn't let them put the stuff on his engine and they were disturbed.

One night about 8:00 pm the yard job was switching up at the top end of the yard. I was sitting at the YM's desk when the engine pulled up to the office. I knew they weren't through with the work, so I went out to see what was going on. We had an extra crew that night who were not exactly the "cream of the crop". In came John Kocielko, the foreman. John was a trouble maker from the word go, and he had that "I'm here for trouble look".

He said, "That engineer won't take our signs and we won't work with him anymore. I asked John specifically what was happening. He said they were trying to shove a cut of cars and

would give Hall a sign to move ahead and he would shove a bit and stop, claiming he couldn't see them.

I got up in the cab and asked Hall what was wrong. I don't remember what he said, but I said, "Let's go back up where you were and we'll see why you can't take the signs. Hall made this later-to-be notorious reply.... **"Now I'm going to tell you something, BUSTER"**.... I stopped him right there, told him to take the engine back to the yard office and that he was out of service for insubordination.

I called George Voss at home and told him what I had done. George was not a great one to back up his officers, so he gave his usual "I mean to say, are you sure you should have done that". George was always "tough" in the second-guessing of proper discipline.

The upshot of the affair was that we set up an investigation for Hall, or tried to, but we couldn't ever find him at home to deliver the notice. We did finally have one, where I testified and the switchmen testified, and Floyd was again fired. I later heard that he got back to work after a considerable length of time. Long after I had escaped to the Freight Claims Department. I heard that he was running a switch engine in the Blue Island yard and pulled a similar trick at not moving when he was supposed to. Carl Holt, the then Terminal Supt. who later became president of the Roscoe, Snyder and Pacific went up to see Floyd in the cab as I had done that winter night at Joliet. Floyd is reported to have told Carl. “You run that office and I’ll run this engine”. I believe that his firing was permanent that time.

After my little “encounter” with Floyd, you can guess what my nickname was. Ed Ledebuhr and Ed Seeley never let me forget it.

WHEN BAD THINGS HAPPEN TO GOOD AND LOYAL LONG-TIME EMPLOYEES: “THE COVERUP”

Chet Ballard came from a family whose male members most all worked for the Rock Island. His father was an engineer as were several of his uncles and cousins. They were all top notch, quality, conscientious employees and Chet was no exception.

Chet was probably in his late thirties to early forties and was mostly working the engineer’s extra board. When a man got promoted from fireman to engineer or from brakeman to conductor it was almost like starting over again. As a fireman or brakeman with lots of seniority you could hold the choice jobs, but when you got to be an engineer or conductor it was back to the extra board and the lousy night jobs on switch engines with little or no overtime.

I don’t remember whether Chet had been forced on the night Joliet yard job or was there just relieving an engineer who was off, but there he was.

In earlier Sections, I have described the “middle connection” which was a crossover from the yard track “No. 1 above” to the north main track. We used this for westward trains which had only a few cars to set out or pick up. The

mainline switch was a facing point from the west, trailing point from the east.

I can't remember the details of how the near disaster occurred, but somehow some of the fine Joliet switchman had left the inside switch on the crossover lined for the crossover instead of straight down No. 1 track. The mainline switch was, of course, lined for the main.

At Joliet all of the switch engines were headed west and the switching was done, normally from the east end, so a move down No. 1 track westward would normally have had the engine going forward. The crew must have been pulling some cars down No. 1 and Chet apparently was looking back to the east and before he realized what was going on he was through the open inside switch and partway through the mainline switch which was of course, lined for the main. Fortunately he realized where he was and got stopped before he was all the way through the switch, but the damage was done. The bridal rod and the connecting rod were both bent. The engine didn't derail and they got back in the clear.

Ned Barnett, the night YM, went out and along with the crew straightened up the rods the best they could and spiked the switch for the mainline.

When Joe Van Gampler, the day YM came on duty at 6:30 in the morning, Chet stayed around to talk with him and fill out the accident report. He asked Joe if he would hold the report until he (Chet) could "talk to the Trainmaster". Joe agreed to not say anything and he had Ben, "I won't answer my phone at night no matter how much you ring it," Long, the Section foreman, repair the switch. Ben was able to straight up the rods and nothing had to be replaced, and not much time was spent on the project. Joe told Ben not to make any kind of report yet and Ben agreed.

When I came in about 10:30 Joe explained to me what had

happened and who the engineer was. I had never met Chet Ballard, but Joe explained that he was an employee "par excellence" and that if we could avoid making a report it would be the right thing to do.

It had always been my policy to accommodate an employee in trouble, if I thought it was justified and that it would be appreciated. However, running through a mainline switch was extremely serious and could have resulted in Chet being in "deep doo-doo". I told Joe that I was willing to not say anything, the burning question was. "What if George finds out?" If he did, both Chet Ballard and Hedgpeth would be in the DDD.

Later that day Chet came in to talk to me. He explained that he had been an engineer for about 20 years and had never been in any kind of trouble. His record was perfect. He admitted full responsibility for the incident and made no excuses, but said since there had been no expense involved and the switch was back in service could we "cover it up".

I agreed to tear up Chet's accident report, and after swearing Ben Long to secrecy, decided that we would just overlook the matter. I lived in terror for several weeks after that fearing "that George would find out". He didn't.........

Chet became another Ed Dickens in prostrating himself in gratitude before me. He would come in every time he was down at Joliet and thank me. This incident occurred in late 1961 or early 1962. Several years later when Chet had a regular suburban run and I was in the Freight Claim Department and riding the train downtown every morning from Midlothian, Chet would see me on the platform, lean out the cab window, blow the whistle, and yell. His gratitude was unending. I loved it.....

TELEPHONE TRICKS

Bob Willett was the second trick towerman at the MC TOWER. Bob had a son who lived a few miles away at Charleston, IL. Charleston was a long distance call from Joliet. Bob had a habit of ringing up his son during quiet times during

Bob Willett, Train Controller at the MC tower CTC panel with Wes Coppel looking on in this 1947 photograph. Other "MC" controllers were Cliff Witherspoon and Thomas B. Drew. The board covered double track Rock Island territory from Blue Island to Morris, Illinois. -- David Willett collection

his tour of duty on the city phone who's charges, including long distance calls, were paid by the Rock Island. The calls apparently were numerous and lengthy enough to call the attention of Norb Simon, the Tower Supervisor, to the matter. After looking into the matter, it didn't take long to discover who was making the calls. An investigation was held and Bob got some kind of discipline.

Nick Green was the day yard clerk at the Joliet Yard. Nick's normal attire didn't make him an object of sartorial splendor. It was more like "I slept under the viaduct last night and just got up and came to work". He always had a two or three days growth of beard and tobacco juice ran from the corners of his mouth. He was, to say the least, slovenly in his appearance and more slovenly in his work habits. He had worked with Joe Van Gampler many years and Joe took care of him.

At the end of his tour of duty each yard clerk was to make a walking check of the yard and have a fresh check of each track for the new clerk and YM. Nick didn't often get beyond the end of the yard office to make his check. Joe would tell him how the crews were going to switch the tracks and Nick would take the fresh checks he got at the beginning of his trick and line out cars that were gone and draw arrows to indicate cars being moved. His checks were a mess. When the afternoon clerk would come to work, he would just go up and walk the yard and make his own new check. They all complained about Nick, but Joe took care of him and it went on and on.

ANYHOW.... In spite of his work habits and appearance, Nick was a well read man and was possessed of quick wit and a great sense of humor.

Several months after the telephone calls matter Nick called Bob Willet one afternoon and, putting him on, told Bob that Norb Simon, had been down that day looking around. "Well, what did he want, asked Bob?" "I don't really know" answered Nick. "He just asked for the telephone slips and was looking them over when I left". Bob probably spent a few anxious days after that.

SUBSTITUTE POWER

At most points which originated passenger trains in volume and in the days of steam, I believe every terminal had "protection power". That is an extra engine which could be

Fast Forward to 1969 and Norb Simon (right) is now general supervisor of suburban operations. He's pictured with J.A. Pochron, suburban trainmaster and Jack Sparrow, customer relations specialist.

used in an emergency when one of the regular engines went bad order at the last minute. We even had a protector at Blue Island for the Suburban Trains running out of there when I was working as TM there.

Joliet was not blessed with the luxury of a protection engine. 5 suburban trains originated at Joliet each weekday morning. There were five engines to do it with.

It only happened once, but it did happen. One of the regular suburban engines failed at the depot. There was only one thing to do. Substitute the 830, an EMD SW-8 (see photo of one of it's brothers on page 20.) This 800-hp conventional yard switcher had 30 mph top speed. The suburban train rocketed past the yard at an astounding 15 mph without lights or heat and did manage to make it to Blue Island, quite late of course.

They did manage to get a regular engine on there to complete the run.

At Joliet, not only did we not have a protection passenger engine, we didn't have a protection switch engine. Of course nobody at Blue Island thought about returning the 830 to us for the afternoon industry jobs, so we waited for the first suburban run to come in about 5:45 to have an engine to use. The job, of course, got overtime because of a 3-hour late start. George, of course, complained about the overtime, and life continued its normal course on the Rock Island in 1962.

MY QUALIFICATION AS A BRAKEMAN

In researching my archives for some ideas, I came across my qualification slip, written by Conductor L. E. O'Dea (No. 6 on the seniority roster in 1963). The Avoca and Harlan Branches are gone. The Guthrie Center Branch is gone. Atlantic to Winear is now part of the IAIS. Brakeman Jim Hedgpeth is a bit different too.

After completing my physical and rules exam given by TM V. R. (Verlie Ray) Beeson, a former Chief Dispatcher and somewhat of a misfit as a TM, I was marked up on the brakeman's extra board at Short Line Yard (Des Moines). It was about February 2, 1959.

Business was slow and I laid on the board for a couple of days. Finally the crew dispatcher called me and said "by the way Beeson said you have to make some student trips". Wonderful. Why didn't he tell me before I was marked up and I could have had them done.

ANYHOW... It was a trip on the ROCK ROLLER.. This job originated at West Des Moines (Formerly and now

2-7-59

V. R. Buson

Bkm Jim Hedgpeth is O'K on Avoca + Harlan Branches also O'K Atlantic to Winnas + D-Center Branch Ready to Go to Work. Very Good

Cond. O'Dea

My qualification slip as a brakeman and seniority list on the West Iowa Territory, Western Division of the Rock Island

ROCK ISLAND LINES

WESTERN DIVISION

West Iowa Territory

Seniority List of Brakemen — Revised to January 1, 1962

No.	Identy	Name	Seniority
1	3542	Schoonover, H	Jul 28 1923
2	3543	Dunn, T	Jul 31 1924
3	3769	Desmond, D	Sep 2 1927
4	3407	Morehouse, M	Sep 9 1927
5	3803	Osborne, H	Aug 27 1928
6	3773	**Admire, O V	Jul 16 1929
7	380[illegible]	O'Dea, L E	Jul 16 1929
8	3861	Hallock,	Aug 30 1929
9	3841	Daughenbaugh F	Aug 10 1941
10	3839	Nossman, B R	Aug 11 1941
11	3840	Crandell, D C	Aug 12 1941
12	3845	Saylor, B	Sep 20 1941
13	3866	Bright, J	Sep 25 1942
14	5[illegible]	***Guyer, D E	Jul 19 1944
15	5289	Rushing, C S	Oct 31 1944
16	5357	Mackey, C C	Dec 23 1945
17	5380	Richardson, J	Jan 23 1946
18	5384	Estrada, K	Aug 26 1946
19	3493	Bright, G R	Jun 28 1947
20	5338	Wilson, K W	Jul 20 1947
21	5301	Fister, F H	Sep 8 1950
22	4566	Fuqua, D	Sep 19 1956
23	7201	Dean, Sam	Oct 24 1956
24	4415	Koop, K J	Sep 11 1957
25	4416	Stearns, H	Nov 7 1957
26	4418	Atwell,	Nov 7 1957
27	4417	*Todd, K M	Nov 8 1957
28	4421	Dockr[illegible]er, J	Aug 28 1958
29	4422	Dingman,	Sep 11 1958
30	4424	Leazenby, H	Sep 14 1958
31	4425	Rogers, G G	Sep 18 1958
32		***Hedgepeth, J	Feb 12 1959
33	4450	Hall, J	Apr 14 1959
34	4454	Bond, W F	Apr 21 1959
35	4460	Oberender, J	Apr 22 1959
36	4491	Schrader, D	Jun 2 1959

*In Armed Services
**Retired a/c Disability
***On Leave of Absence

currently nicknamed the "trendy" VALLEY JCT.) Called for about 6:30 am with two GP-7's in the 1200 series and about 100 empty gons for rock loading at the quarries at Earlham and Winterset. The rock was used in cement manufacturing at the West Des Moines plants. This move was made over the "new line" completed in 1958 between Earlham and Winterset to replace the old line which came over from the "spine line" south of Des Moines through Martensdale and was extremely hilly and full of curves. The new line was completed in about had some extremely steep hills, but it was, at least, fairly straight.

This day was very long and we ended up tying up at West Des Moines about 9:00 pm.

The other student trips involved two days on the Atlantic Local. This job originated at Atlantic. One day it went east on the mainline to Earlham and worked the Menlo-Guthrie Center branch. The next day it went west to Hancock Jct. and down the branch to Oakland. Then back to Hancock and up the branch to Avoca on the Old Main Line, then over to Walnut, then west to Harlan Jct, up to Harlan and over to Shelby. Another couple of long days.

I was working as a student brakeman, and hence, getting no pay. The head brakeman was a guy cut off at Fairbury and working out of Des Moines. I remember his name, but I won't mention it here....he might still be around. O'Dea didn't like him. It wasn't long before O'Dea found out that I knew what I was doing...He called the other guy back to the caboose and told him to stay there. He put me on the head end and told me that even if I hadn't worked in the territory before, I was better than the other guy. He gave me a favorable recommendation to the TM. Beeson never asked for the slip, so just put it in my file.

All of the above provide a bit of historical documentation. I'm not making all of this stuff up. A little added here and there to add flavor, but most of it is reasonably accurate.

A FEW GLIMPSES OF THE CAST OF CHARACTERS AT JOLIET

I've already told you about Ben Long, the NON-NOCTURNAL, section foreman. His most memorable associate was a scrawny little Mexican guy of indeterminate age referred to variously as "Mexican Pete" or "One Eyed Pete". Guess what....he only had one eye. He could speak almost no English. Pete was the "lamp man". Remember we're still in the days when most all the switches had oil burning lamps. The lamps would burn about 7-8 days on one filling. Pete's job was to keep the founts on the lamps filled. He took his job very seriously. He literally immersed himself in his work. He always appeared as though he had bathed himself, overalls and all, in a barrel of kerosene. He was soaked from head to toe with the stuff. I was always afraid that in the winter when he was around a fire or close to a stove that he would spontaneously combust, but he never did.

Pete was the only section man you could get out at night to sweep switches in the snow or to help with a derailment. He didn't have a phone, so I would have to drive to his house, pound on the door, wait for him to get dressed, and then haul him in the company car to where he was needed. I always put newspapers on the seat before he got in, but the car always reeked for days afterwards. If Pete wasn't sweeping the switches fast enough, the switchmen would yell and shake their fists at him, but Pete just kept on. He never complained. An interesting character.

I've told you about switchmen Ed Sealey, the joker, and Dick Doolin the overtime king. They were the good guys.

There were others not so good...As in most places most of the not so good guys worked nights where they could sluff off.

There must have been a building boom going on around Joliet in the early 60's as many of the switchmen had jobs as roofers or had roofing crews of their own. They would work their "other job" during the day and then come to work at the yard at night and want to sleep on the job. One of the most notorious was Elmer Cargle. Elmer couldn't "tawk pawne". He also was missing his two front teeth and had an irritating way of punctuating each sentence with a little laugh at the end. I named him "the giggler". Elmer also had ulcers. One day one of his cohorts was getting a can of pop out of the machine and asked Elmer if he wanted one. Elmer's reply was "Nope, I can't drink that carbureted stuff. The king of the roofers was John Kocielko. A short little polish character. He did quite a bit of roofing in the nearby town of Platteville. Apparently one of his brother switchmen was trying to get a job in Platteville which John viewed as his own territory. I heard him tell the other guy, "Stay out of Platteville". That became the cry whenever you saw John. John's full name was John S. Kocielko. I came to refer to him as Jack S. Kocielko (remember Jack S. Phogbound in Lil' Abner). He never caught on....

Then there were THE BROTHERS ANDERSON...FRANK AND FORREST. Never have I seen two men, both with the same parents who were so different. Forrest was an excellent switchman. He could get more work done in a short time than any switchman I ever saw. He was awfully rough though. He made his moves count and accomplished much in a short time. He had to be allowed to take a longer "bean hour" though or an early "quit" or he would slow down. This drove George crazy and I had to be careful how I handled things. Frank was the opposite. He wasn't overly bright, and made up for it by being slow, bull headed and extremely prone to injury. He had more personal injuries than all of the other switchmen combined. Frank was tall, well over 6 feet. One day he stood up while coming out of the back door of a switch engine, banged his head, and had to go home injured and was off several days. He had been fired several times, for being injury prone, but he was still there when I left. Forrest and Frank occasionally worked together. Frank would continually argue with Forrest about the work, but Forrest would just send him off to the side and do two men's work.

Sam Haynes was THE WATKINS MAN. Sam was a very conscientious switchman, and really tried to do a good job, but he was slow. He would make 3 moves when one would do. Sometimes he would work with Forrest Anderson and it just frustrated Forrest no end. Sam drove a red 1952 Ford Panel Truck to transport his WATKINS products. I don't know how much business he did WATKINS-WISE, but I was always having to get after him to get about his switching and do the WATKINS STUFF off the job. We did buy some WATKINS Products from him from time to time, as did most of the other employees. In getting a job started, when Sam was foreman, I would tell Sam what needed to be done. He would always say. Now....Jim here's what I think I'll do...He would then proceed to slowly tell me about it. I didn't care how he did it, but he seemed to think that he had to give me all the details.

Nick Green, the nightmare of non-sartorial splendor was the day yard clerk who was described in an earlier section. His cohort in the yard office was Joe Carrigan, the Operator. There was no "operating" to do, but Joe kept some car records and he was supposed to keep up the JUMBO BOOK. All of you who know what a JUMBO BOOK was, report to me. If you don't know and want to know, ask me...If you don't know and don't care you don't need to say anything...As I mentioned before, Nick was quite well read and liked to use polysyllabic (sic) words just for fun. He and Joe would go out and walk round the yard on their lunch periods "in search of the elusive

Acridiidae"...Look it up if you don't know what it is. Nick's kids, which he had in great number, were notoriously ill behaved. Nick was Catholic. One day he reported that some of his kids had broken some windows in a church. His comment: "Of course it would have to be the Baptist Church".

TOWERS AND TOWERMEN Part 1

Joliet was home to three interlocking towers. C & A TOWER, located just across the Santa Fe and GM&O tracks east of the Joliet UD. This tower was named for the former Chicago & Alton, predecessor, in that territory, of the GM & O. In the long-standing railroad tradition of never changing the name of a location, track or railroad it remained in 1961 and I believe the tower is still in use and still referred to as C & A tower.

C & A controlled the RI, SANTA FE, GM & O crossing as well as the connecting track from the RI to the GM & O-Santa Fe. It was a busy place, but normally operated fairly smoothly and didn't interfere with the freight yard operation at all. The towerman at C & A was kind of a yardmaster at the coach yard and oversaw the storage and switching of the suburban trains. The day towerman was Joe Arriagano a very excitable fellow with a high-pitched voice. I don't remember any of the other operators.

"J" (EJ & E) tower was located about a mile or so east of the C & A Tower where the EJ & E mainlines crossed the Rock Island. We had little to do with this operation, except call in panic to get him to lift the derail when a car got away from the yard crew headed down the lead toward the J crossing. If there was enough time and no J trains were approaching he would let the runaway across the J unscathed. If that happened, a call would be made to the MC (Michigan Central, predecessor to the New York Central Joliet) to see if they could let the runaway into their stub end yard for retrieval by the switch engine.

MC (Michigan Central) tower controlled the Rock Island mainline from MP 48 to Blue Island. It also controlled the Michigan Central/RI crossing. A bit more about the (NYC) operation later. The RI train dispatchers at Rock Island controlled the territory from Rock Island to MP 48 and it was MC tower from there on into Blue Island.

The territory was two main tracks signaled in both directions with power crossovers near the AMOCO SPUR west of Rockdale, at the C & A TOWER at JOLIET UD, at MP 35, at MOKENA and at the Blue Island interchange tracks with the GTW, IHB and B & O.

It was a busy territory and required a high degree of skill to interweave the morning and evening suburban rush with the mainline passenger and freight trains. Of course when a freight train had to make a set out or pickup at the Joliet Yard it complicated things a bit which leads up to the men who ran the tower.

The regular first trick towerman at MC was Cliff Witherspoon. Cliff was an enormous guy with an enormous ego also. His most famous story was that for many years Bennie Wells (the infamous General Manager) had relentlessly pursued him to take a Trainmaster's job. The pursuit allegedly became so intense that Cliff had to keep home window shades drawn in the evenings, because Wells would drive by his house or come to his door.

Anyhow Cliff was "mister congeniality" to cooperate with the train crews. When an eastbound train had a setout to make at the Joliet yard Cliff would put him on the north track to save handling an extra set of hand thrown switches to come over from south track to the north track and into the yard. Cliff would also call the freight trains and tell them where the "dummies" (suburban trains) were so that they could avoid passing between the "dummy" and the station platforms at New Lenox, Mokena and other suburban stations. I always got along well with Cliff, but Norb Simon the Supervisor and other officers didn't like him at all.

Bob Willett was the regular second trick towerman. I have spoken of him before in connection with his illicit long distance phone calls. Bob was OK. He was fairly cooperative, and didn't have a whole lot to say.

The third trick at MC belonged to the Train Dispatchers through an agreement worked years ago between the towerman's union and the ATDA. It was always a young dispatcher and changed frequently.

HERBIE SCHENK was the swing man and a pain to all he came in contact with. Herbie, one of those even-tempered guys, who was mad all the time. He was almost totally incommunicative with the train crews and seemed to relish giving them a bad time. While Cliff would do all possible to make the trainmen's work easier, Herb did all he could to make it harder. i.e. Train 44 was the eastbound Silvis - South Chicago train. It usually got to Joliet in mid to late afternoon. He was a local and usually had quite a few cars to set out at Joliet and we almost always had cars for him. Here's how it would go.

"Train 44 callin' the MC Tower"....repeat about 4 times before Herb answers

"MC TOWER"....in grouchy monotone

"Herb we got a Joliet setout, can't you put us on the north track???"

"NOPE."...silence

"Why can't you put us on the north track?"

Long pause....."Got the dummy comin'...."

He could have put the dummy on the south track at MP 35 and crossed him back over at the Joliet UD or just left him on the South track but that wasn't the way Herbie operated.

When 44's conductor brought the bills in, I always had to listen to a harangue regarding Herbie's non cooperative nature.

I would occasionally try to talk with Herb, and he was always civil enough, but always had some plausible reason why he couldn't do what seemed to be the best thing for the operation. I talked with Norb Simon about the situation, but he wasn't able to do anything either so it just went on and on.

The MC (the NYC) came into Joliet from the east, I think from East Gary. They ran one train a day into Joliet in the late afternoon. They always had two GP's for power. I never saw their train, but it couldn't have been much. The only industry they had was Ruberoid, a roofing manufacturer. I think that they had a road crew which brought the train in and the yard crew who did the switching which consisted only of the Ruberoid plant and making deliveries to the connecting carriers. They never called before they came, but we expected them anywhere from 6 to 8 pm. Here they would come with their one or two covered hoppers shoving the cars ahead of the engine so you couldn't see them. Occasionally we would be making a late delivery to the J with a heavy cut going down the lead and encounter the MC chugging up the lead. They usually backed up and got out of the way. The conductor would bring the bill(s) into the office and I would have them stick their one or two cars into a track to be switched and they would depart -- a shadow into the darkness.

FOOTBALL SPECIALS AND SUBURBAN EQUIPMENT

Here in Lincoln, I once saw a BN passenger train at "Ira's crossing." Not knowing what it was I contacted one of our experts who of course knew all about it. The train consisted of all of 3 sleepers or coaches and two bi-level suburban cars painted in the new BN Corporate colors.

I commented that this was probably the first time bi level equipment had been in Lincoln and he told me that during the last years of the CB & Q trains had brought bi-level equipment out from Chicago to run on the Omaha-Lincoln football trains.

This reminded me of how the Rock Island handled football trains to Iowa City. The Rock Island Football Specials were run into Iowa City from Omaha, Des Moines, The Twin Cities, and the Quad Cities (Davenport, Rock Island, Moline).

On Friday night after the suburban trains had completed their runs. The 2700 series suburban cars (the AC depressed door cars) were either made up into a DHQ (Deadhead Equipment Train) pulled by a couple or more of the Alco Suburban engines and run to Rock Island to be used as the Quad Cities train. Or most often the suburban cars were placed on the rear end of train 41 at Blue Island and we had to add ours at Joliet.

There had to be suburban engines sent to Quad Cities for these trains, because their lights could only be powered by the generators on the suburban engines. I may be wrong about this since these cars had the Waukasha engines for the Air Conditioning and they were self-sustaining on electrical power also.

They did, of course, need steam for heat from the locomotives. What was really exciting was when, late in the season, after the weather had turned cold that the cars would come back into Joliet on the rear end of some freight train about 3:00 am on Monday morning frozen up and with trash piled up to seat level inside. We had to get out extra coach cleaners and carmen to get these cars ready for the 5:30 start of the suburban rush.

It was the usual practice, year round, to use the suburban engines for freight power on the weekends. It was understood that they were not to go beyond the Quad Cities, but occasionally some Chief Dispatcher got overly ambitious and some units would get to Des Moines and getting them back for Monday was ticklish. Also there were only certain units which were to be used in freight service.

The reason was that, as manufactured, the Alco prime movers had relatively soft crankshafts, not being designed to be subjected to heavy loading for long periods of time. Some of the units had been in for overhaul and had "hardened" crankshafts installed. These were OK for any service. Occasionally a "light duty Alco" would get sent out and overworked in freight service. Inevitably it would be towed in with a thrown rod because of crankshaft failure.

A DAY IN THE LIFE OF THE JOLIET TRAINMASTER

The old memory bank is getting a little thin as I try to recall more incidents and activities during my Joliet days before starting to relate my experiences after being promoted to the "big time" in the Blue Island-Chicago Terminal. So we'll try to get one more section out of Joliet.

My officially assigned hours at Joliet were supposed to be 10:00 am to 10:00 pm. Of course anyone who railroaded during that era knows that all operating officers were always on duty and expected to be available 24 hours each day 7 days each week. The Rock Island, however, thanks to D. B. Jenks, started a program sometime before I came on that Officers were to receive 2 days a month off. Shortly before I arrived it was increased to 3 days. That's not 3 days a week.. That's 3 days a month. Many of the Superintendents, I was told, were not good about giving their officers their days off, but I will say, in spite of all his other idiosyncrasies George Voss did give us our days off. I don't recall ever missing any. But other than that it was minimum of 12 hours 7 days a week.

I related earlier, that shortly before I went to Joliet that the only supervision on the yard operation was by a single yardmaster who worked 10:30 pm to 6:30 am. The appointive agent was supposed to look after the yard operation from 6:30 am until the Trainmaster came in about 10:00. Previous to my regime, the agent was L. C. Foster who was a good operating man and was well liked by the crews. Shortly before I came, Foster was transferred to Des Moines as Agent and W. J. Jackson was appointed Joliet agent. Joe was somewhat less than ambitious and knew little to nothing about running the yard. Theoretically he was supposed to take care of things when I wasn't around, but it was like the proverbial "pushing with a rope" to get him to do anything. He spent most of his time sitting in his office at the Freight House, looking at his clean desk.

Anyhow...let's presume a normal previous day which let me get away around 11:00 pm the night before.

I would get up around 7:30 or so, have breakfast with my wife and then 6-month old son. He is now almost 43 so you can see it's been awhile. We lived in a rented house in a rural area about 5 miles east and 5 miles north of Joliet. After eating breakfast I would mow the yard or take care of other home-type chores and about 10:00 would drive the company car, Car 804, a black plain Jane 1960 Ford 4-door equipped only with heater and company radio. I was allowed to take the car home since I was on call 24 hours, to the yard office in the east edge of Joliet.

Usually things were pretty normal when Joe Van Gampler the long time night YM was handling his 6:30 am to 2:30 pm 6 days a week shift. Joe almost never laid off and consequently things during the day were in good shape. Joe was very good to tell me about anything that went wrong and was also good to take care of problems without bothering me. He used to say "I told Jackson, but "he wouldn't do nothing" so I just waited till you came down.

Usually the first thing that greeted me was a very late 46 (the Peoria-Chicago) local that always had a Joliet set out and cars to pick for Blue Island. As related in previous tales, it was supposed to do the local work between Joliet and Blue Island, but since it was always late and the Rock Island was always short of power, we would give him a New Lenox or Mokena set out and before he got out of town the dispatcher was on the phone yelling that "those engines stand for No. 81 or the GSX so "run" the work and get him in." I've told about cars of lumber making 4 or 5 trips between Joliet and Blue Island before being set out.

After 46 got out, Joe would be bemoaning how much work there was in the yard and how he had to use "Pinky" to deliver the "J's" and other chores before he could go over west of the river and switch the Caterpillar Plant and other industries. Pinky Rogers was probably the most conscientious employee I have ever known. He was at least 60 years old, probably older. Everybody over 45 seemed old to me then. Shortly before I was transferred, the doctor disqualified him from service for some physical defect. It was a very sad day. Pinky came in and was actually crying….Begging me to see if I could arrange

for him to keep on working. I don't remember the outcome, but think that he had to take his retirement….

After Pinky's job had gone west, I would go over the yard checks, looking for delayed cars. I had to also review the engine hours and overtime which George continually yelled about as well as writing nasty letters asking how he was going to "explain all this to MANAGEMENT". About that time Joe would be checking up on No. 44 (the Silvis South Chicago local) 44 was usually on short time with a big train, and little power. His usual horses were something like the 48-50B. A couple of the old pencil draw F2's. Here it would come dragging along at MP 43 calling the Joliet Yard, telling us he had 35 cars to set out and what did we have for him???.. He was usually just about in time to tangle with No. 81 (the Denver Hotshot due out of Blue Island at 11:00) and 91 the GSX (Gold Streak Express due out at 11:30). Right ahead of No. 3 (Golden State due out of La Salle St. at 1:00 and No. 7 (Rocky Mountain Rocket due out at 2:00 pm) along with assorted "dummies". If Cliff the Towerman were on duty, he would put 44 up the north track for his set out and weave the other trains around him. If Herbie was on duty he would keep 44 on the south track waiting until all the rush had cleared and then 44's crew would have to handle a main line crossover to make its move. Then the "crabbin' and the bitchin' and the gripin' and the moanin'" would start.

If 44 was going to have to set for awhile, the plea.. "Can't we set out in the SHAW TRACK. The SHAW TRACK was an auxiliary track on the south side of the two main tracks. It had a power switch on the west end controlled by the E&JE Tower and a hand throw on the east end. If we had let 44 set out there and go on, then the yard engine would have had to go over and get the cars and drag them across the mainline. That would take at least an hour in most cases. I made the mistake of letting that happen once, and caught so much flack from the yardmasters that I never did it again.

After 44 would get his setout and pickup made he would get back on his train, pump up the air and try to get started.

Usually he could get out of town and make it about five miles to just east of New Lenox where Mokena Hill started. Usually 44's Conductor would say.. Well Joe you better plan to shove us to Mokena. Joe would always assure them that they could make it. After they got going we would anxiously wait for the 15 or 20 minutes it took to get part way up the hill. Sometimes they would make it, but often if the weather was bad and the power short the cry would come. Joe...we're stalled. We would then have to send the switch engine the five miles to try to get them over the hill. Sometimes it was enough and sometimes it wasn't. It cost an hour's time at least of the engine being out of the yard. The switch crew got a minimum of hour's punitive time for the work which was no work at all.

By this time, I would have gone down to the Freight House, stopped at the Cuckoo Clock Drive-in for a hamburger and done some other miscellaneous chores.

About 1:00 I would get back to the yard office and confer with Joe as to what industry car orders we had and how far along his switching was and how Pinky was doing getting back from his Caterpillar run.

Joe and the yard clerks would take switching orders all morning long from the various industries. Remember we had one day engine and two afternoon engines that did generally all industry switching. There was lots of business at Joliet.. The industry switch lists and car orders were very high tech. We kept a pad of "clip paper" with 2 carbons between the three top sheets. When an industry would call in, Joe would note the industry Number. Caterpillar was 240.. Chicago Gravel was 243 etc. When the orders were taken they were stuck on a board with a nail driven through it for each afternoon engine.

About 1:30 Nick Green, the daylight yard clerk would come in and quiz Joe as to what switching he had done and where he had put what cars. All of this to save Nick from actually going up into the yard and making a check as he was supposed to do. As I related before, Joe let him get away with that stuff and Nick would take the checks he had gotten from the night clerk...draw arrows and line out and generally cobble these "hard cards". When the afternoon clerk came on the first thing he would do was to go up in the yard and make his own check.

About 2:00 Joe would "get out of the chair" and I would get in. If things were not hectic I would tell Joe to go on home. He would say OK, but usually ended up hanging around answering the phone and talking to the clerks and switchmen.

At 2:30, in would come Sam Haynes or whoever was the foreman on the afternoon yard engine. I would give him the yard checks and have him tell me where he would make Sealy and Doolin (The afternoon industry switchers). Sam would say.... "Well Jim here's what I think I'll do......." He would then proceed to do this 'thinking out loud' and Sam was not a fast thinker.... I would then finally get him out of the office and started with his work.

By that time Ed Sealy (the ultimate joker) would be in for his work lineup. His first job was to deliver the EJ&E out which was anywhere from 20 to 80 cars. After he got done with that delivery, It would be time for me to see how Sam was getting along with making up the trains for the industry jobs. Hopefully he would have Sealy's train made up so he and

"Winfield" could get out to do their work ahead of the suburban rush.

Dick Doolin, the foreman of the 3:59 pm far west job would come in about 3:50 to get his work lineup. His job took the most time and he always made from 2 to 4 hours overtime. He had to switch Caterpillar, Chicago Gravel and then go on west on the mainline to what we called the AMOCO SPUR. This spur generated some really good traffic for the Rock Island. Amoco had a large refinery which would produce 3-5 outbound cars each day. There was also Freeport Sulfur Terminal. This industry brought in raw sulfur by barge on the Illinois River, melted it with high-pressure steam and then loaded it into tank cars. This was very high revenue stuff and was extremely heavy. There was also a paper company and several other industries on this line.

The Freeport Sulfur was a commodity that needed to be moved promptly. Train 45 was Blue Island - Peoria local which got to Joliet about midnight or later. The Sulfur routed to Freeport Illinois via the RI Peoria interchange. In order to expedite this traffic he would have to come back to the mainline with the sulfur cars and put them on the rear end of No. 45. This would cost an extra hour or so of overtime. If we didn't do it then these high revenue loads would be delayed 24 hours.

After getting the two industry jobs out of the yard or seeing that they were going to get out OK, I would make a dash to the freight house in car 804 to pick up the waybills and any mail for the yard office. This would consume about 45 minutes to an hour. Sometimes the bills wouldn't be ready and John Haley, the Agent's Chief Clerk would work overtime. More "criticism" from George... Back to the yard office with the bills so that the afternoon clerk could get them lined up for our pickups which would go out that night.

Usually about the time I was trying to get the industry engines out of the yard, the "J" would come with a delivery for us. They were supposed to call before they came and we always did for them, but they didn't often return the courtesy. Sometimes Sealy's engine would meet the "J" engine coming up the lead. The "J" always had a big train and they were coming out of their main terminal yard so they couldn't back up. We had radios on the engines, but none on the cabooses, so with much cursing and arm waving Sealy would back up into the yard and let the "J" in. They usually had one of their old Baldwin switchers and took delight in seeing how slow they could move since the crew was on overtime. Often they would stall, and have us completely blocked out.

The hottest commodity in the J Delivery was from 4 to 8 cars of groceries from The Jewel Tea Company in Barrington going to stores in Minneapolis-St. Paul. These groceries were loaded in empty reefers going back home and were fairly high revenue plus being freight that had to be expedited. They were picked up by Train 41 (the South Chicago-Silvis train leaving South Chicago about 6:00 and getting down to Joliet about 8:00 to 10:00. I'll detail how we did his setout and pickup later on.

After getting the bills to the yard, getting the industry engines out, and being sure (if that's possible when dealing with switchmen) that the yard engine was getting on with his work, I would head home for supper.

Usually my short evening at home was interrupted by several calls from the yard regarding various matters, especially if Sam was the foreman. He would call me two three times to let me know what he was doing...

After eating, I would call the yard and see how 41 was doing as I wanted to be there when it arrived. If it was going to be a bit late I would stay home for a little longer, especially if I had a good engine foreman.

About 7:00 or later I would head back to yard to be around when 41 got in to be sure that his pickup was ready and that the switch crew wasn't goofing off any more than we could tolerate.

DISASTER WITH THE COMPANY CAR, AND GEORGE CHECKS UP!

As mentioned in past chapters, the RI Company vehicle assigned to the Joliet TM was 1960 4 door Ford sedan...Black Maria type. The Joliet Yard was located behind and beneath, it seemed, a cemetery and reached by a road which dropped steeply off the cemetery access road into which a large tree protruded and required a conscious effort to steer around it.

It was a “dark and snowy day” and the road was packed with ice and snow...I had been out on some emergency run and came whizzing down the cemetery road...wheeled down off onto the yard access road and began to slide toward the offending tree. There was nothing I could do, but brace myself for the crash and it came. Fortunately the only damage was a significantly crumpled right front fender and headlight. Fortunately the car was drivable.

Fearful of reporting the matter to George, I wired him the details.. Fortunately the car was drivable. The next day “came the call”... I was greeted by George’s voice to query. “I mean to say, who do you think you are??? Barney Oldfield”. He OK’d getting the car fixed and the matter ended rather quietly although razzing from the switchmen and yardmaster continued for quite some time.

George wanted all of his officers and employees to think that he was on duty 24 hours each day and never took time off and that he expected all of his employees to operate the same way.

It was “time change time”... This was a semi-annual crisis which occurred the last Sunday in April and the last Sunday in October when the time changed from Central

Standard to Daylight Savings or back. You old railroaders will recall that the railroads didn't recognize daylight savings time, but merely scheduled the trains to run one hour earlier or later as the case might be, when the time changed.

After 1966 when daylight savings time became official, the employee timetables showed the same time as the public timetables, but this was 1961 and there was always an hour difference during daylight time months on the railroads.

It was Saturday night October 28, 1961... The time changed at 12.01 am Sunday October 29,1961. There apparently had been some kind of crisis earlier on the Saturday evening and I was still at the yard when Ned Barnett, the night YM, came on duty at 10:30 pm. Normally on Saturday night, when we had no industry engines working and there was no other excitement, I didn't hang around. This night for some reason, I was still there and stayed around talking to Ned until after midnight.

About 12:15 am or thereabouts, the company phone rang and Ned answered it. He said "yes he is...just a minute". Ned handed the phone to me and said "It's Voss for you"...

George of course didn't expect me to be there and when I answered all he could think of to say was his usual greeting... "HEDGPATH!!...?"

"Yes sir..."

"Well, I mean to say do all of your crews have the new timetable?"... When I assured him that they did, he continued

The boss himself, GHV, George Voss Superintendent of the Chicago Terminal Division with division headquarters in the background.

his usual "quiz program" until he had stumped me on something and then ended the conversation.

Later when I was at Blue Island about 9:30 pm George would call the yard office from his company car No. 84 (dubbed "Car 84 where are you"?) and ask a few inane questions of the yardmaster attempting to create the impression that he was out on patrol checking up on things. After the conversation the yardmaster would usually comment. "Well, George must have gone out to put the company car in the garage before he went to bed".

Since I'm on the radio topic I might as well continue and describe a comedy routine that often took place about 6:30 am each morning at Blue Island.

Mel Voitik was the night terminal yardmaster at Blue Island... Mel held the No. 1 position on the Yardmasters

Seniority Roster, but he preferred to work nights "when nobody was around to bother you". Mel was probably about 60 years old and was a contemporary of George as far as switching and yardmastering. As with all railroads then and now there was some effort made to maintain proper decorum and procedure on the radio. Mel didn't hold much with proper radio procedure .. He was the old school--- and did just about what he wanted. He was an excellent YM and nobody criticized him much to his face.

Here would be the routine taking place anywhere between 6:30 and 7:00 am as George was driving from South Holland to Blue Island... "Rock Island Car 84 calling the Blue Island Yardmaster... The proper response for Mel was "Blue Island Yardmaster.. go ahead." Car 84..."

What took place however after the call from Car 84 was .... "Yeah, come in George". George, trying to teach by example and intimidation would repeat the call. The response "Yeah... Come in George".... This could go on three or 4 times with neither changing the response...

Finally George would give up and say... "Mel what time did we make the 'Harbor'". (Perishable delivery to the IHB due at 4:00 am). Mel would give the time and then George would query on the "Trunks" (Grand Trunk Western) B & O's... "the House spotted???" (It never was)... "What time did the 'pigs' (TOFC) get out for twelfth?" and on and on.

It was a constant source of amusement among the trainmasters to answer the radio "Yeah, come in" as Mel did.

In Part two, we'll move to my tenure at Blue Island and discover the various and assorted characters among the switchmen and clerks...Including a fellow we will call "Casper". He was the ultimate "Casper Milquetoast" who reportedly commented to one of the trainmasters that, "He didn't think it was right that he had to sleep out on the back-porch when his wife's boyfriend stayed overnight"

Montgomery "Monte" the day transportation clerk one of whose first duties each morning was to call in the "nothing to report, report". This became a glaring example of RI inefficiency when the new management took over in 1964 and was reported across the railroad. Then there was Iver Waltham (just like the watch) and relief transportation clerk who was just a bit balmy.

Part II

CHICAGO DIVISION OPERATIONS

Office Hours

Telephones for communication with Dispatcher or Block Operator are located as follows:

MP 15-48	MP 23-17	MP 30-35	MP 36-11	MP 41-6
MP 16-11	MP 23-50	MP 32-29	MP 36-35	MP 41-30
MP 16-44	MP 28-36	MP 34-6	MP 37-6	MP 42-15
MP 18-11	MP 29-34	MP 35-17	MP 37-47	MP 43-18
MP 20-13	MP 29-43	MP 35-27	MP 41-3	MP 43-26
				MP 43-33

Blue Island	Continuous	
Midlothian	6:00 A.M. to 3:00 P.M.	Daily Except Saturdays Sundays and Holiday
Oak Forest	6:00 A.M. to 3:00 P.M.	
Tinley Park	6:00 A.M. to 3:00 P.M.	
Mokena	6:00 A.M. to 3:00 P.M.	
New Lenox	6:00 A.M. to 3:00 P.M.	
Joliet	7:30 A.M. to 4:30 P.M.	

F. J. GARNER, Ass't. Supt.
F. G. VESTAL, Trainmaster
B. L. LOWERY, Trainmaster
J. P. HEDGPETH, Assistant Trainmaster
L. C. BROGDON, Assistant Trainmaster
J. E. BERGSTROM, Master Mechanic
L. C. LONNEGREN, Road Foreman Equipment
J. W. BURKE Road Foreman Equipment
N. P. SIMON, Tower Supervisor Ass't. to Trainmaster
} **Blue Island, Ill.**

R. J. VINSON, Assistant Trainmaster, } **Joliet, Ill.**

M. R. EWING, Chief Dispatcher
D. M. MARTIN, Assistant Chief Dispatcher
G. R. WILLIAMSON, Assistant Chief Dispatcher
C. R. GIBSON, Assistant Chief Dispatcher
} **Rock Island, Ill.**

H. C. McENTIRE,
H. F. FURMAN,
A. R. MYERS,
G. W. OLSON,
J. N. HARDIN,
R. C. FEE,
W. W. WEST,
C. J. YORK,
C. J. STOFFER,
R. L. THOMPSON
J. F. CORDER,
} **Dispatchers, Rock Island.**

Chicago Division 18

THE BLUE ISLAND YEARS 1963 - 1964
TRAIN LINEUP

In answer to a question on the RITS (Rock Island Technical Society internet list) I posted the following:

"Well let's see what an old Chicago Division Trainmaster from 1961-64 can do with his memory and an October 1961 Chicago Division Timetable.

Let's run a calendar day out of Blue Island, South Chicago and Joliet

First thing out was No. 59, the PBX (Piggyback Express) due out of Blue Island at 2:00 am. This train carried, from the head end: Denver (DRGW connection) auto parts, TOFC etc., Sandown (RI Piggyback ramp) trailers and tri-levels, Council Bluffs TOFC, Des Moines TOFC, Silvis TOFC. The theory was that the train be worked from the rear end at all stops. At Sandown, RI Piggyback ramp and point where the RI cutoff left the UP the TOFC and tri-levels were left and the head-end of the train went on to Denver North Yard where the DRGW handled things.

2nd out of BI in the early a.m. if there were enough cars to run one was the Red Ball Pickup. This train, in theory, hence the name, was to handle short cars from Joliet to Silvis, picking up the "hot loads" (remember years ago expedited freight carried a RED BALL symbol on the waybill to designate high priority) at Joliet, Morris, Seneca, La Salle, Bureau etc, to arrive at Silvis in time to be humped for No. 81 and 91 the next afternoon. It may have worked that way in times past, but normally the RBPU didn't get to Silvis in time for that to occur.

Burr Oak Yard at Blue Island, Illinois, Chicago Terminal Division Headquarters

No. 43 was the hotshot out of South Chicago, due out about 7:30 am. He carried stuff from eastern connections which were delivered at South Chicago during the night i.e. Erie, NKP, PRR, CSSB, C & O, This train normally filled at Blue Island. This had to be done by switch engine from the rear end and was accomplished at Purington (north end of Blue Island yard). This train would sometimes pickup at Joliet, but normally he went straight through to Silvis. Again the idea was for 43 to be at Silvis and humped for No.'s 81 and 91 (next out of Blue Island)

No. 81 was due out of BI at 11:00. This train carried Denver and beyond hot stuff with lots of tri levels and trailers. His train was made up of stuff delivered at BI in the late night and morning hours by IHB, Grand Trunk, PRR (at Englewood), B & O, CEI (at Oakdale). He was "filled out" with mty PFE's to whatever the tonnage and car limit was that day.

No. 91 Gold Ball Express was due out about noon. Gold Ball was the symbol for California expedited cars. He carried hot traffic for Kansas City, and the Southwest (Dallas, Ft. Worth and Houston) and California. Lots of auto parts. Ford Motor Company would call the BI yard office each day with car numbers determining if these cars made No. 91. If they didn't and should have woe betide the guilty party.

The afternoons at BI were quiet with perhaps a drag being run if there were enough cars left over at 81 and 91. In later years after the Langdon Management took over the term "drag" was eliminated and the new term was "Overflow Manifest" (OFM).

No. 41 was due to leave South Chicago about 7:00 pm. He was usually filled at Blue Island as did 43. He picked up at Joliet, there were usually 5-10 "grocery" loads out of Barrington IL for Minneapolis as well as some other hot stuff.

Next up out of Blue Island was No. 45. This was the Peoria Local. He usually got out about 10:30 or so barring complications. He carried Peoria and connections cars and usually had a pretty good size train. This train did the local work on the North side between Blue Island and Joliet. "North side" meaning industries which were best worked from the North Track. Tinley Park was the most common one.

This train picked up at Joliet, Morris, Ottawa, La Salle and Bureau.

Next and last out was No. 93. He was the Texas Hotshot with lots of good stuff for Ft. Worth, Dallas and Houston. Texas Shippers trailers were the most critical item on this train.

Piggyback transfers were handled between BI and the 12th St. Ramp by switch engines. For outbound traffic a pull was made fairly early in the evening for No. 93, the hot run sometimes there were two, from 12th St. to BI were made later in the evening. If memory serves me correctly the cutoff time for trailer delivery at 12th St. was 11:00 pm and tied down was to be done by 11:30. This was nightly crisis. If you were lucky the transfer got out of 12th St. by midnight and if you didn't stall too many times getting out at 16th St. you got to BI by 1:00 am. The flats were supposed to be blocked at 12th St. by DRGW, DENVER, Council Bluffs, Des Moines, so that the train could be put together more easily at BI. There were also trailers from the BI ramp that had to be folded into the train. It was a real panic right until 2:00 am.

It was after 59 got out that the Trainmasters took their lunch break and plotted their alibis for George Voss's early morning "quiz program".

Here's the inbound (eastbound) scenario.

After midnight the focus and building crises focused on the inbound perishable trains.

These trains consisted of perishable traffic handled at that time mostly in PFE ice reefers. The trains were, by Number 98 which was the train from Ft. Worth-Dallas, 84 and/or 82 (I can't remember which one was the day and which the night). This was the Omaha train and carried mostly meat and PHP (packinghouse products.) No. 94 which was the Cedar Rapids train with meat and PHP from Wilson at Cedar Rapids and other connections. These trains were consolidated or separated as time and traffic varied. Most of the perishable was destined for eastern connections via IHB and had to be delivered by 4:30 am to make the cutoff and avoid a chargeable delay to the Rock Island.

The big panic at this time of the day was the delivery to eastern connections. A missed connection was almost as bad as delay to outbound No. 91 or 59.

There were also perishable deliveries to be made to the Grand Trunk and sometimes B & O.

There were also always perishable cars for CPT (Chicago Produce Terminal) and Wood Street Potato terminal which had to be delivered "jiffy quick".
This was about it for inbound high priority traffic for the morning. There could be as few as 1 or 2 perishable trains, or as many as 5. It all depended on how the traffic was and how Silvis put the various trains together.

First on the later early morning inbound lineup was No. 46, the Peoria Local. He left Peoria around 7:00 pm or so and did local work all night coming east picking up at the aforementioned stations between Bureau and Joliet. To this train also fell the local work on the South Side between Joliet and Blue Island. The most notable of this was Oak Forest Lumber. What would happen on regular occasions was that a car of lumber for his business would arrive at Blue Island from the east or west. It would be then sent to Joliet to come back on 46. 46 would get the car at Joliet and after he would leave Joliet the dispatcher would call BI yard and say that "we need those engines (normally two geeps) for 81. BI yard would then call 45 on the radio and tell him to "highball" Oak Forest. [As indicated earlier] The lumberyard owner after seeing his car go by 2 or 3 times would get a bit unhappy. This happened pretty regularly.

The inbound South Chicago trains were 42 and 44. 42 was kind of a hotshot and came east in the morning as I recall. He carried the good stuff for the eastern connections to be delivered that night. No. 44 was the plug and did local work between Silvis and Joliet with lots of pickups. He usually ended up in South Chicago in the late afternoon or early evening.

As to the road switchers, and having not worked at any locations between Joliet and Silvis, my memory is not real good, but here's what I remember. Larry Blanchard get on here and correct me.

There was a switcher at Morris. This was normally one of the little 44-ton center cab jobs. There was an engine at Marseilles, or perhaps it worked out of Ottawa handling Marseilles. There were at least two engines working out of Ottawa on first and second trick. There was an engine at Seneca which handled the DuPont plant and other industries. I'm not sure whether there engines assigned at La Salle or not. There were lots of industries between Joliet and Bureau in the time you wanted to know about, and all of the engines were busy.

RE: Peoria trains. Nos. 45 and 46 ran between Blue Island and Silvis, daily except Sunday. No.s 47 and 48 ran between Peoria and Silvis on the same kind of schedule, so there were two inbound and two outbound trains from Peoria each weekday. There was also a Bureau Turn which worked out of Peoria and took care of the industries between Peoria and Bureau.

Also in the picture during the late 50's and early 60's was the RIP (Rock Island and Peoria) line local tri weekly between Silvis and Peoria via Lafayette. Also running were an almost daily Lafayette turn, out of Silvis to take empties to the mine at Lafayette and bring in the loads. This coal moved in gondolas mostly. It took 16 hours plus to handled this kind of traffic over the creaky railroad between Orion Jct. and Lafayette.

Gone shortly after I arrived at the RI were coal mines (open pit) at Atkinson and Annawan which required daily turns out of Silvis.

Well, maybe this was more than you wanted to know, but I took it as a challenge. There's probably few "mis-recollections" in here, but that's how I remember it.

Subj: Blue Island

Date: 6/11/2002 7:31:05 Am Central Daylight Time

To: PSHedgpeth

Sent from the Internet (Details)

Hi,

Good to hear from you and you may have to give your clinic as a fiction because no one would believe half the things that went on there. I have a 50th High School reunion that weekend in Niagara Falls, New York, even giving up a Purdue football game to go. It would have been nice to see you and some other Rock Islander's.

We have a daughter in Evanston and from the Dan Ryan the Rocket House and Car Shop areas look the same, even Root St. Tower, but I think there are only 2 tracks in place of the 6.

I'll give you a couple tales of my nights at the Island. We'd had a terrible week and the suburban trains were all froze up, late and annulled so about 4 AM in walked himself and Garner. About that time Bobby Vinson, Trainmaster at Joliet called in and said the Banker's engine had a boiler failure and to notify GHV. He also added he'd been working on it all night. With that info I told him George was out in the front office to call him out there. When I got out there George was through the ceiling and told me to get Louie and the protector engine and go rescue the Bankers. I went down and found Louie and told him and he said we couldn't as it was a contractual violation for us to do it. I told him that I'd have the line up and be at the depot registering and getting our orders. He went up to the office and in no time at all I heard the Alco protector throttling up and we ran light to Joliet Union Depot where the Bankers had just arrived from Rockdale. We double headed to save time and Louie succeeded in getting by the New Lenox platform and had to back up. Louie said he'd buy breakfast when we got in. Going into La Salle Street a froze up Dummy was backing out with a freight jeep and as we neared the post I saw Himself pacing back and forth. I told Louie to skip breakfast and caught an outbound Dummy. I think that was one of the many short 15 hour nights. Needless to say one of the Supt.'s letters came out about the suburban trains.

We also had a young Out-freight carman that was always late or a no show and the Car Depot would do nothing to correct or replace him. One night he was working the rear end of the Redball Pickup and we were forever pumping air and no set so I walked back with the car foreman and found him sound asleep in a bunk. We made the air test and I told the Conductor to let him sleep and put him off at an open station, I recall that was Ottawa. George raised hell with me the next day, but I told him I'd tried to handle it with Stan Globis to no avail so did it my way.

A guy should have a left a diary as it was an education at the Island. I hope you find your write up and sure that you'll have a good clinic.

Doug W.

More from Doug:

Hi,

The line up looks pretty good as I remember. As far as the locals there was a Joliet Bureau Turn and a Peoria Bureau Turn, both 6 days a week. The switch engines on line were Morris, Seneca, several Ottawa, La Salle and Depue. The switch engines could go light to adjacent towns, but the road crews had to transfer the cars. Work trains that were working just at one station were manned by switch crews and outside of yard limits by road crews, they could work through a town with an assigned switch crew. Silvis also ran a train of shorts east that arrived at Blue Island with traffic that 46 couldn't handle.

Later though service added 57, a GMC train to the U. P. at Council Bluffs, 87 a Cedar Rapids and Minneapolis hotshot. 57 was the hottest of the hot and if very light could be filled with California General Motors Autos. They ran right behind 91 so that filled out the daylight shift pretty well.

That's about all I can think of now.

Doug W.

ROCK ISLAND INTERMODAL

TRAINS magazine carried Ed Ellis' column entitled, INTERMODAL BUSINESS: CHANGING COURSE. Several comments within the article sent me thinking back to Intermodal (then called Piggyback) on the Rock Island.

In opening his piece, Ellis comments that "Change is driven for odd reasons".. i.e. managers on new assignments seem compelled to change things". He quotes a former AMTRAK executive as saying "He saved the Chicago and North Western $50,000 by closing the Des Plaines commuter coach yard and then saved another $50,000 by reopening it". Ellis then goes on to speak of how the intermodal (piggyback) concept originally included ramps at any city, no matter how small, which could possibly generate some piggyback business... Which probably came out of a boxcar (my comment)... He sites examples such as a CNW ramp at West Point Nebraska.. RI had a ramp at Lincoln, as most of you know, as well as at such other minor points as Iowa City, Newton, and even Oakland, IA. Since the early day ramp consisted of removing one set of trucks from an old flatcar and shoving a little dirt around it and sticking it out on the end of a spur or freight house track, there was little cost involved. The thrust of Ellis' article is that since "industry has ruralized itself", that perhaps railroad terminal facilities should be decentralized as well. He comments on the high cost of drayage which drives carriers out of many markets.

I have nothing of a philosophical or analytical nature to offer regarding Ellis' thoughts since the purpose of this piece is purely entertainment (maybe), but only memories of how things were in the early days of piggyback on the Rock Island.

In Chicago, the Rock Island had probably the most convenient, if horribly small, cramped and inefficient terminal of any carrier...It was located at Taylor St., approximately

Roosevelt Rd (12th St.) A few blocks west of La Salle St. This was in the heart of the freight, express and mail houses which had served the Chicago railroads in time past.

There were four or five loading tracks set up for circus style operation (no cranes) with a center track running down the middle of the ramps and on about 2 blocks further north, ending at Polk St. Each track would hold about 4-5 doubles (80' cars) or about twice that in singles (40' cars made from old flatcars or gondolas). The facility was located just north of the twelfth street coach yard where the suburban cars were stored during the day.

The ramp "office" was the old scale house where dray vehicles were weighed in LCL days. The loading foreman was an excitable fellow named Nick Carigianni, and the general overseer was a former trucker named Oliver Harriman. The operation was under the control of and used the equipment provided by the Rock Island Motor Transit Company. That Rock Island subsidiary maintained its equipment to somewhat less than exacting standards (even less exacting than its parent company). Each loading tractor could be described, in the words of Highball Wilson of LIFE ON THE HEADEND FAME, as an "animated scrap-heap"

The loading for the evening departures, No. 93 (Gold Ball for California) due out of Blue Island at 11:00 pm and the PBX No. 59 the hottest train on the railroad at that time, due out of Blue Island at 2:00 am would begin in the early evening and grow in intensity toward the 11:00 pm cutoff for the PBX.

We had to block the PBX thusly from the headend: Denver (D&RGW), Denver (ramp), Council Bluffs, Des Moines. The yardmaster at 12th Street would attempt to get the loading

foreman to load each track by destination i.e. Denver's on one track, D&RGW's on another track, etc. so that when the

Two photos of the 12th Street Piggyback Yard in Chicago

loading was completed, the train could just be doubled up and depart 12th St. The biggest problem encountered in attempting an efficient loading pattern was that Nick would not leave a trailer on the ground when he didn't have another immediately available to match it for the same destination.. Consequently when Nick was in charge there would be trailers for all destinations on all tracks... A switching nightmare. Harriman was a bit more rational and could at times be quite cooperative, but he wasn't always around and sometimes suffered from the brown bottle flu.

To switch the 12th St. facility was extremely difficult since you were always working around curves with long strings of flatcars. It was a fairly common occurrence to hit the ramps with something less than a velvet touch, and if the touch was too unvelvet-like the ramp would be disabled. When this happened, Nick would immediately pick up the phone and call Harriman at home or on occasion George Voss who would instantly call me demanding to know what had happened, most times were before I even knew about it.

Leonard Ellul, relief yardmaster, certified stand up comic, and tormentor of Nick often worked the 12th St. job. His comment was that "when we hit the post, it knocks the phone off the cradle and into Nick's hand and automatically dials Harriman's number".

One night we were short of cars and didn't have any empties to spot to the ramps after the loads were pulled. This always created an instant crisis...Nick expected empties to drop from the sky immediately after the loads were pulled out. Nick would call the yard office about every five minutes demanding to know when the empties would be there. We had to keep a running log of what time each track was pulled and when it was re-spotted... It was CYA every minute. Finally after Nick had called several times about the empties he wailed "I've got

Above: The hottest train on the Rock Island, the PBX.

Right: Inbound pigs, from Blue Island.

Left: Loading a trailer Circus train style.

all these men here with nothing to do". Ellul's reply "why don't you have them pull weeds?"... Within 3 minutes George was on the phone to me demanding to know what was going on.

After the loading was complete, Nick or Harriman would call the YM and say "tied down at 10:45 or 11:03 or whatever it was. That, in their thinking, ended their responsibility... Many times, because of Nick's convoluted loading, it would require 45 minutes to one hour to get the switching done and the loads lined up. On a heavy night, the train would stretch from Polk St. (800 South) to about 14th St. Well over one half mile. The power usually consisted of an 800 hp switcher (grossly inadequate)

After the air was pumped up and tested, no small task with the train strung out that far around a series of curves and through the 12th St. coach yard, it was time to make an attempt to get under way.

If I was at 12th St. (which was my usual spot) I would race up to the shanty near the turntable at 14th St. and yell into the tower line intercom "Hello 16th St." 16th St. controlled the St. Charles Air Line and the IC West Line to Omaha.

The response "Yeah 16th St.."

Me "Got the pigs at 14th St. ready to go to Blue Island with 23 cars."

The reply: "Got a guy goin' around the WYE with 50 cars then I can take him."

I would step out of the shanty and give the engineer a sit still signal.

The tower would want to know what engine and how many cars since if the power was small (it usually was) and the train was big, it was likely that the train would stall with the headend across the diamond at 16th and the rear end hanging back down in the yard. It wasn't a pretty situation, since there was no radio on the yard caboose to indicate whether it was OK to back up and make another try if the first one wasn't successful.

Anyhow, when the 16th St. tower man gave me the OK, I would run out and line the switches out of 12th St. onto track 5 and swing a vicious highball to the hoghead. On a good night with a dry rail and a decent engine and engineer the hotshot would creak and groan and squeal its way out of 12th St. for the 45 minute to one hour run to Blue Island.

Occasionally on Saturday when the tie down was completed early and the suburban trains weren't running, we could get "superpower" for the transfer run. The ideal combination was 400 and 401 back to back. These were Fairbanks Morse engines which had been re-engined with EMD power (1500-hp per unit – 3,000 total compared to the 800 hp we usually had.) The 400 and 401 were used in suburban service during the week. The ideal engine crew was Engineer Tom McHenry and fireman Tony Orseno. One Saturday evening they made the run from 12th St. to Blue Island in 22 minutes... That was passenger train time.

After arrival at Blue Island, it was necessary to cut in the pigs from the Blue Island ramp plus any tri level auto racks and other hot loads left over from No. 81 and get the train out by 2:00 am.

It was an every night but Sunday adventure. When there was delay it was US vs. THEM.. US was Rock Island Operating dept. Them was Rock Island Motor Transmit (the loading crew). We would show "late tie down" as delay and RIMT would show slow loading because of no cars or slow switching. It was a fun time, but in 1964 I escaped to the

It's the fall of 1964 and new U-25-B No. 224 and its brothers were assigned to hotshots like the Denver-Chicago DCX which is shown here in Council Bluffs, Iowa. 2500-hp per unit.

In 1966, more and more important freights began originating at South Chicago shown here rather than at Blue Island. F-7A 114 and GP-7 1264 were still very much alive!

Freight Claims Department and became an observer and critic of the operation rather than an active participant.

TOWERS AND TOWERMEN Part 2

An article on towers in *Trains* Magazine set me to thinking about the tower operations on the Rock Island in the Chicago Terminal Division. So here's a section of more tower memories.

On the Chicago Division these were the towers located between La Salle St. Station and Joliet... about 40 miles.

Polk Street Tower: This facility controlled the trackage at La Salle St. Station and the east end of the 12th Street coach yard. The tower, during my time in Chicago, was manned by a Train Director and two lever-men during the first and second tricks and probably just one man during third trick. The Train Director was actually the yardmaster of the depot. He decided what trains would pull into what tracks and where the outbound trains would be made up. He directed the activities of the two switch engines. A New York Central Engine and a Rock Island Engine. Just as an aside it seemed that some of the primary requirements of a towerman were that he be, excitable, able to shout at top decibel range of his voice repeatedly, and be athletic enough to run up and down the length of his domain rapidly and heave the armstrong levers. Several of the Rock Island towers were still of the Armstrong variety, although I believe that Polk Street was all electric or electro-pneumatic.

An additional feature of the Polk Street Tower, which was alluded to in passing in the *Trains* Article portion relating to the Chicago Union Station Towerman was the TELAUTOGRAPH. This device was forerunner of today's FAX machines. The towerman would write a message on the pad of the TELAUTOGRAPH and the same message would appear on a similar piece of equipment in the stationmaster's office. When the stationmaster or gateman would see 90///10. He would know that NYC No. 90 was going to be made up track No. 10 and would hang up the appropriate gate signs and inform the REDCAPS. I was always fascinated with the TELAUTOGRAPH, and had intended to write about it sometime, and the *Trains* article sparked a bit of memory to prompt this. I wouldn't be surprised if the same device is not still in use at the Chicago Union Station.

The next tower out, located about one mile from La Salle St. was 16th St. tower. This tower controlled the crossing of the Illinois Central line running to Omaha as well the St. Charles Airline... one of the several "paper railroads" in the Chicago area. The tower featured a small shack at its base where a man was stationed at all times whose function it was to count the cars of all movements moving over the Airline and keep those records. Each road using the Airline was charged so much a car or wheel.

Root Street Tower: Located about 35th Street or so. This was strictly a NYC operated facility on the east side of the 6-track complex. Root Street controlled movements in and out of the NYC Coach Yard and around the CJ (Chicago Junction) WYE leading to the stockyards industrial district, CPT (Chicago Produce Terminal) and Wood Street where reefers of potatoes were unloaded. Passenger train "Backups" out of the 51st St. Coach Yard were turned on this wye before backing down to La Salle St. Station.

A word here about the trackage. Beginning about 16th St. going (timetable) west, (geographically) south the furthest east track was No. 1. This track was used exclusively by the NYC for both coach yard-depot moves and by inbound road trains. 2 was the next track over and was used by the NYC for outbound NYC depot-coachyard moves as well as by outbound mainline trains. Track 3 was the inbound RI mainline.. Signaled only for eastbound traffic. No. 4 was the outbound RI mainline signaled only for westward moves. Track 5 was signaled in both directions and was used by the RI both for switching moves and for express suburban trains which didn't make many station stops. Track 6 was non-signaled and used mainly for switching and transfer moves. Tracks 1 and 2 became the NYC Mainlines at Englewood. Tracks 3 and 4 became the Rock Island mainlines at Englewood. Track 5 at Englewood became a running track for express trains, and switch movements. Track 6 ended at 61st Street Tower, just north of Englewood. Track 5 from Englewood to Gresham was a runaround track for express trains and was used for switch engine transfer moves when not otherwise in use. From Gresham to Purington (east end of Burr Oak Yard) track 5 was not signaled and used for switching and transfer movements.

Back to the towers. The next tower south of Root Street was 45th St....This most ancient structure which handled movements in and out of the Rock Island Coach yard 47th St. It was removed from service in the mid sixties. It was a brick edifice literally hanging over the edge of the Dan Ryan Expressway. When the excavation was done for the Dan Ryan was done, it came right up to the foundations of the 45th St. structure. Each time, I observed this place, I wondered what kept it from toppling over onto the Dan Ryan. I was never in 45th St. Tower, but I understand that it was the most ancient of the ancient and its operation was a sight to behold involving toggle switches and hooking up wires. Its functions were consolidated with Root Street tower at its demise.

61st St. Tower was next in line...located about 1/4 mile north of the Englewood Station where the Rock Island and NYC parted and where the PRR crossed. About all that 61st St. did was control entrance to track 6. It was 100% armstrong and quite small and cramped.

Next was Englewood Tower located in the southeast

quadrant of the RI-PRR crossing, south of Englewood Union Station. It controlled the RI-PRR Crossing and the interchange track (RI-PRR) and Englewood teamtrack.

Gresham Tower was about 5 miles south of Englewood at the Junction of the RI Suburban Line and the mainline. The train director at Gresham was the real "nerve center" of the suburban operation. He controlled trains into and off the Suburban Line and trains onto and off of the RI South Chicago Branch over which trains of the B&O operated between South Chicago and Beverly Junction (91st St.) If anything went wrong at Gresham...everything stopped. There was a signal maintainer stationed at Gresham who was always "at the ready" during the morning and evening suburban rushes.

91st St. Tower...located at 91st St. about 2 miles west of Gresham where the Suburban Line turned south for Blue Island. This was a very quiet place as his only function was to let B & O trains on and off the Rock Island.

Going on down the RI mainline the next tower was Washington Heights whose only function was to control the PRR Panhandle Division crossing and the Rock Island. It also had some control over switches into Chicago Bridge and Iron plant.

At the south end of the Burr Oak Yard was Blue Island Tower. This was brand new facility replacing the old tower in the early 1960's as part of the Cal Sag Calumet River navigation project which went on over 7-8 years. BI Tower controlled the south entrance to Burr Oak Yard as well as the interchange tracks at 139th St. where interchange was made to the IHB, B & O and Grand Trunk.

The author took this photograph of the Blue Island depot and tower in 1990. Metra handles the commuter trains and the Iowa Interstate makes use of what is left of the yard on trackage rights on the CSX from Bureau Junction, Illinois.

Looking north in Joliet along the Santa Fe/ GM&O main line with Joliet U.D. off to the left and the Rock Island main line crossing west to east in this view of CA tower.

MC (Michigan Central) Tower at Joliet, previously alluded to controlled the railroad from 139th St. to MP 43 west of Joliet.

C & A (Chicago and Alton forerunner of GM&O) tower controlled the RI, GM&O-ATSF crossing at Joliet Union Depot.

The tower operation was of a magnitude and importance that a "Tower Supervisor" was one of the division officers. N. P. (Norb) Simon was the man. Norb, was another of George's mortal enemies. In George's eyes, no towerman ever did anything right (sometimes it seemed that way) and in Norb's eyes no towerman ever was in the wrong...It made for some interesting conversations......

The towers communicated with each other through an intercom line. The Trainmaster's office could tap into the line and listen...It was a good way to keep track of what was happening on "your railroad". No train orders or CTC was involved...From MP 43 west of Joliet to La Salle St. Station trains and engines just moved from tower to tower on signal indication.

The two Rock Island Color Pictorial Books have pictures of most of these towers. Sadly enough, I wasn't doing much if any picture taking during my Chicago Division stint, so I have none.

Some of the towermen were really colorful characters, although most of them I never saw in a person, but only knew through phone conversation.

There was Cliff Witherspoon the day man at MC who had to keep his home window shades drawn and doors locked, because Benny Wells was always coming 'round to beg him to give him a trainmaster's job...There was Bob Willet at MC of illicit long distance call fame. Herbie Schenk at MC the most cantankerous of all towermen.

Joe Arriano at C & A was the most excitable and competed with the best for talk at high volume. John Griny (I believe he was 2nd or 3rd trick leverman at Polk St.) took his honors also for loud talk and an excitable nature.

It seems that little time has gone by since the interlocking towers which were so much an integral part of the operation during my time 40+ years ago in Chicago are now almost extinct.

I'll end this section with a brief vignette which has only to do with towers in that it happened in front of the Blue Island depot and tower. The Red Ball pickup was the mainline local which was supposed to get out of BI about 4:00 am. He was always overloaded and underpowered and late. If you didn't get him out before the suburban rush he would have sit and wait until 8:00 or so.

One morning with a couple of shaky old units like the 40 and 43b, the towerman in a burst of generosity tried to let the Red Ball out of the yard between suburban trains about 7:30. He got about a quarter of his train out past the depot and the tower. The south end of the yard blocked including the street crossings when both units died...what a catastrophe.

George showed up and said "HEDGPETH...."I mean to say....if you would get these trains out on time this wouldn't have happened…" Who can argue with logic like that?

GEORGE IS STRICKEN....HEDGPETH IS PROMOTED WOE.. WOE.. WOE

It was summer 1962... probably July. Each month there was a Division Staff Meeting when all of the Division Staff Officers were summoned to George's Office on the second floor of the Blue Island yard office for about two hours of grilling for the purpose of creating maximum embarrassment for those who were on George's "list", haranguing on whatever the current "management" criticisms were, and general harassment of the "troops".

These meetings were usually scheduled to begin at 9:00 am and generally broke up by about noon. Joe Jackson, the Joliet Agent, and I usually drove up together for the meetings.

On this day we arrived shortly before 9:00 am and noted an ambulance parked outside office. We climbed the stairs and upon entering the general clerical office outside George's "Sanctum Sanctorum" we were greeted by all the assembled gathering and George's Secretary, Francis (she was a master of wit and sarcasm.. I hope I can think some of her comments concerning George as we go along). Francis said, nodding toward the north stairway.. "They just carried Him out of here on a stretcher". It was thought that GHV had suffered a heart attack or some such debilitation. I can't remember much other than Oliver Thurston, Assistant Supt, dismissed the meeting, which really had never started and as Dizzy Dean was fond of saying "the players returned to their respectable bases".

The upshot of the situation was that GHV was diagnosed to have suffered a possible heart attack, although I heard him later comment that he had eaten half a cantaloupe for breakfast that morning and that was the problem. George was a continual smoker and a chewer of La Palina Cigars and was definitely a "TYPE A" personality although he was quite trim, and didn't appear to indulge in any abnormal vices other than continually striking terror in the hearts of those who worked for him.

Within a few days the following changes were announced: Oliver Thurston, Assistant Superintendent was made Acting Superintendent, Ralph Parker, Trainmaster and continuing tormentor of GHV was made Acting Assistant Supt. J. P. Hedgpeth was made Acting Trainmaster at Blue Island and R. J. Vinson, who was a former yard clerk at Little Rock was made Asst. Trainmaster at Joliet.

The long dreaded move to Blue Island had come. Although with George away it wasn't bad. The promotion didn't last long however...I don't recall exactly how long, but I went on vacation about Labor Day and when I returned Ralph Parker informed me that I had been "bumped". George hadn't yet returned, but they had brought someone else back, and the end of the world had come. Nights at Blue Island...there was nothing worse unless it was winter at Manly, Iowa which fortunately, I never inherited.

The night job at Blue Island was my lot from September 1962, until I was liberated by J. H. Gilfillan (I'll relate more on that later) in April 1964. Two dreaded, cursed winters in the Chicago Terminal. Rather than try to be chronological from here. I'll just relate some incidents that happened during this period. I can generally separate the various "happenings" as to summer or winter. The winters of 62-63 and 63-64 were vicious with lots of snow, and below zero temperatures. Which, given the decrepit nature of most of the Rock Island's equipment, made for some interesting times, for night TM at Blue Island. I still have copies of some of the correspondence which I received from George during my period of exile.

Before relating any specific happenings let me tell you about some of "cast" that made up the "players" in the nightly Chicago Terminal Saga played out between Joliet and La Salle St. Station 7 nights each week.

The afternoon yardmaster at Blue Island was Al Simnick. A relatively young YM and was quite competent. I was recently informed that Al is now with METRA in the Chicago Area. Al did an excellent job handling his shift. The main events at this time of day were getting No. 45 (the Peoria train) due out about 10:30 pm out, and getting organized to run No. 59 (PBX) Piggyback Express, the hottest train on the railroad that time at 2:00 am. The 12th St. YM was Jim Vieke a southern Indiana native who was competent and a bit excitable. Switchmen of note were Edward (Dizzy) Waite on the afternoon Clearing Job. This was a transfer run which went to work at 3:00 pm at Blue Island and whose only mission was to deliver cars to the Belt Railway of Chicago at Clearing yard and on the way set out cars for the B & O at 87th St. The job usually had 75-100 cars and one of the Rock Island's "finest" for power.. The 759 or 760. Subject to breakdown at the most inopportune times and places. The job was supposed to "couple" tracks 15 and 16 (cars for Clearing and B & O), pump up his air and go. You wouldn't believe the stalling and delays which could plague this job. The car inspectors would blue flag the track and diligently seek out "bad orders", which had to be thrown out. You could have thought that he was going to get on the mainline at 70 mph. They usually managed to fiddle and fool around until 8:00 or 9:00 pm before getting out. One day my predecessor Earl Seal (of reefer behind the caboose fame) decided that, come what may he was going to get that Clearing Run out in decent time. He arranged to have another engine couple up the tracks and put the ground air in the train so that could be taken care of. All the crew had to do was double track 16 to 15 together and go....

With Earl standing literally over them they did manage to get ready and go in record time, something like around 4:30 or so. Earl thought that he had really done something.

Later in about another hour or so the YM said to Earl,

"what's that backing in at Purington (the north end of the yard). Would you believe that they were backing back into the yard. After somewhat recovering from his apoplexy, Earl ran down to the caboose to see what was going on. The reason for the return......Dizz forgot his gloves....

There was no way to win......

Other engines working in the afternoon were the "house job" It required literally 3 switch engines each day to handle the Blue Island Freight House. Remember we're still in LCL days. The afternoon engine would pull all the tracks and was supposed to switch out the outbound loads for the trains that night. Normally he would just shove the "setbacks" back in and the "night house job" was supposed to re-spot and reset the house. This normally didn't get done though, and one of my earliest calls in the AM would be from Mike Dell, the Blue Island Freight Agent, and a very excitable Italian, shouting in the phone: "Hedgpeth...did you know that the house isn't spotted...I've got 100 men here with nothing to do.

His next call, of course, was to George and then it was "I mean to say," Hedgpeth why isn't the house set... do you know how much that costs ME for all those idle men?" and on it went.

The night yardmaster was Mel Voitik. Mel was No. 1 on the yardmaster's seniority roster, but he preferred to work nights away from George. Mel was a totally focused man. His entire efforts for his 11:00 pm to 7:00 am trick was to get the perishables delivered to the IHB, and Grand Trunk. The Rock Island was big in the fresh fruit and vegetable business from Southern California and Arizona and we would get 2 to 5 perishable trains every night. We'll talk more about these later.

As time for the perishable trains drew near along with the 4:30 am cutoff, Mel would become more and more agitated. The night Infreight Engine was usually the first to "get out on the hill" (139th St.) to get the perishables off 84, 94, 60 and the other trains and get it delivered. You could hear Mel shouting over the speaker system. Elmer (Benkowski, night infreight engine foreman) Elmer...Elmer... "Shove that cut in and give me a call". That was Mel's label... "Shove that cut in and give me call".

Among Mel's lieutenants were Vester Nelson, Coach Yard Engine Foreman. His job was switch and lineup the suburban coaches. He finished the night by making a perishable run and lots of overtime. Tom Beno was the Foreman on the Englewood job. An industrial switcher with not too much work and lots of overtime. Another was George Dunn, who later died a tragic death, having both his legs cut off in a switching accident. There was also Bridgeworks Job whose only mission was to switch Chicago Bridge and Iron. They were an afternoon job and managed to consume 12-14 hours in doing little. Also an Eastside Job...another industrial job with lots of opportunity to hide out and stall for OT.

Some of the transportation clerks (these guys were the trainmaster's clerks on a 24-hour basis) who were supposed to keep track of incoming and outgoing messages, taking calls for the trainmaster, and provide information to the Chief Dispatcher: were Vern?? (I can't come up with his name) who was crusty, but good help. Vern was the regular afternoon man. Then there was Iver Waltham (just like the watch). Who was borderline flaky. And then there was Monte who had worked night trick for years and had bid in the day job shortly before my arrival when the former day clerk retired. Monte was the author of the "NOTHING TO REPORT" "report" which became famous when the Langdon management took over in 1964.

Let's get in a happening or two: It was in the dead of winter...1963 or 1964. No. 9 due out of La Salle St. at 10:00 pm had Business car 99 with O. W. Limestall, VP Operations on the rear end. It was cold, cold. Louis Lonegran long time Road Foreman of Engines was on the head end.

As No. 9 left Englewood, Louis is on the radio calling the Blue Island Trainmaster: "The air is froze on the rear end of this train...." What would happen is that the moisture accumulating in the trainline would freeze and slow down or stop the flow of air to the rear of the train. Not a healthy situation. Can you go over to the roundhouse and get a can of alcohol and meet us at the Blue Island Depot. Of course I could. I ran down the steps, leaped into the Signal Supervisor's Jeep, which we used for transportation at night. The signal supervisor was Russ Carle. Russ didn't really like us using his vehicle, but it saved having another vehicle on the division. More (much more) on this vehicle later.

Anyhow, I called the Roundhouse Foreman, who had heard the call on the radio and told him I was coming right over. He had a can of alcohol ready. The can was of the variety used at old time filling stations to fill radiators. It had a long spout. The foreman placed the can on the front seat of the jeep and I raced over to the depot just as No. 9 came to a stop in a great cloud of steam. There was a saying that "most railroads run the steam through the trains, but the Rock Island ran the trains through the steam". Anyhow Louis dropped off the engine along with the fireman. We managed to break the connection behind the 2nd unit and get the spout of the can into the air hose on the head car. We did manage to get some of the alcohol into the airline, but most of it got spilled. I guess it worked, as No. 9 did make it to Rock Island that night.

Here I was "with a college education" in my suit, complete with fedora hat, wrestling a can of alcohol on a depot platform in -20 degree weather. Such was the life of a Rock Island

Junior Executive in the 1960's. They didn't have that stuff in the pamphlet they handed out when recruiting on college campuses.

A NIGHT WITH THE RPO'S

The advent of real winter weather and my comments regarding RPO's and RPO Clerks brought to mind one of the most miserable and frustrating nights that I ever spent on the Rock Island. It took place in January either 1963 or 1964 after I was "promoted" from Joliet to the "big time" in the Chicago Terminal under the direct supervision of G. H. Voss. I'm inclined to think that the year was 1963, but it really doesn't matter....the misery and frustration are timeless.

Just recently I was rereading one of my favorite railroad books LIFE ON THE HEADEND by Pete Adams who was a Canadian Engineer. Some really great stories in this book, published 1956. To open one of his episodes Adams says: "One of the more interesting features of railroading is its latent yet ever-present capacity for springing the unusual or unexpected on you. You jog along for weeks or months in a placid groove and then abruptly the routine is shattered and you emerge from it afterward with a memorable experience". I certainly would add my "AMEN" to that statement. There is no other industry, in my opinion, where the situation can instantly deteriorate from relative serenity to utter chaos literally in seconds. While I wouldn't classify my trainmastering at night in the Chicago Terminal as "jogging along in a placid groove", the point is that the situation can turn down in a hurry and the results of the downturn can be devastating and widespread.

To set the scene, No. 9 was the westbound *CORNBELT ROCKET* due out of La Salle St. Station at 10:00 pm. No. 9 at that time carried normally one or two coaches and a Des Moines sleeping car. Trained directly ahead of the passenger

equipment were two RPOs. These were normally the shorter 60-foot cars (I believe). The balance of the train consisted of a working express-baggage car and several cars of storage mail and express. Also included were 3 to 5 cars from the NYC due to arrive on their mail train around 7:00 pm or so. This train terminated at Englewood and these cars which were called "CITIES" and were brought down in the NYC's usual leisurely fashion by a switch engine. There were normally three cars of Council Bluffs Mail and two for Des Moines.
Anyhow...the operation, which was pretty much the same for all passenger trains was that the coaches and sleepers were brought down from the 49th St. Coach Yard with the road engines. These were known as 9's, or 7's or 3's or 5's (as the case might be) "backup". The engine crews went on duty at the 47th St. ROCKET HOUSE, coupled onto passenger equipment, normally with the engines on the North (geographical) or East (timetable) end of the train as though the train were going to head into La Salle St. Station. The move then was that the equipment went north out of 47th St. pulled around the WYE at Root Street, heading west toward the Stockyards and then backed around the north leg of the WYE and shoved back down to La Salle St. with a switchman pilot on the rear end controlling the movement.

Normally with number 9, the RPO's were supposed to be taken down to La Salle St. in late afternoon or much earlier in the evening than the "backup". Which was supposed to go at something like 8:30. The regular move was that 9's backup would consist of the road engines, usually two units, one or two coaches, and the sleeper. The RPO's which, theoretically had gone down earlier, were placed on one of the station tracks for loading and sorting of mail. The Clerks would man these cars earlier in the evening and begin loading and sorting the mail. Later after the backup came down, the road engines were taken off and moved to an out of the way location and one of the depot switch engines (there were two, one RI and one NYC on all three tricks -sounds unbelievable now doesn't it? But this was 1963 and the passenger business was still pretty much what it had been in the 50's), would tie the RPOs onto the coaches and sleepers.

Sometime after the backup had arrived and the RPO's were placed against the coaches and the head-end equipment put on, the units attached and the steam cut through, the time was probably approaching 9:00 pm. As I patrolled or prowled the platform that frightening night, I was accosted by the Chief RPO Clerk in the usual pleasant and polite manner which was the mark of the calling and informed that one and perhaps both of the cars was not heating properly and that if it wasn't fixed, he was going to "lock up the car. If we couldn't get the heat working the result probably would have resulted in a huge fine for the RI, and perhaps JPH might need to seek other job opportunities.

The carmen fiddled and fiddled, but nothing seemed to work and the clock continued tick away towards 10:00 pm and departure time. Of course there were no spare RPO's available which could have been used. Then the thought occurred to somebody that No. 10 was about due in and we could grab his RPO and use it.

In the meantime the mechanical foreman from the 49th St. Coach Yard had shown up. His name was Harry ?? --his last name escapes me -- a nice personable young man recently transferred up from Little Rock. He was, of course, delighted with the arrangement and soon after threw over his promotion and returned to more pleasant "digs" in Arkansas. Anyhow Harry couldn't do anything with the RPO's either.

No. 10 arrived, probably around 9:00 pm.. We brought the depot switcher against his rear end, preparing to switch out the RPO as soon as it was unloaded. No. 10 at that time carried a "round end" observation car and guess what.....Nothing had been coupled to the rear of that car for a long time. The air hose was completely clogged with ice and snow and there was no way we could handle that train from the rear end.

After fiddling with that situation for sometime, we decided that it was a lost cause. The next moves have been lost in the mists of time, but eventually we came up with one of the 80 ft RPO's which the RI had rebuilt from NYC coaches back in the 50's. Whether it was the car out of 10's train or whether it came from somewhere else, I don't recall. Anyhow we set it out on one of the station tracks and the engine went to put the rest of the cut someplace else. I was standing near the RPO when I noticed it begin to roll away toward the south. I ran and caught the car along with Harry and tried to use the handbrake, but it was frozen solid with ice and away we went making like an "advance No. 9". Fortunately the Polk St. Tower operator who controlled all the movements in and out of the depot spotted the runaway and lined up the switches for a compatible route and called the 12th St. yardmaster for a clear track. He headed the one car- two man runaway into one of the coach tracks at 12th St. and we got her stopped in the yard and tied down. The depot switcher came out and retrieved us and brought us back to the depot.

About this time I thought that a call to George would be in order so I did. I Informed him of all the difficulties, telling him of the RPO Clerk's refusal to go with an unheated car and asking whether we should leave the RPO, the clerks, the mail or some combination thereof. George replied with his usual "Oh I mean to say you can't do that". You can't run that train without the RPO's. Keep after it and let me know. The rest of the night is a blur, but I was calling George about every half hour. I learned that you had to do that to provide some measure of CYA, since if you didn't he would always say, "I mean to say Hedgpeth...why didn't you call me". And he would tell "management" "That trainmaster just didn't let me know what was going on so I could tell him what to do".

The upshot of the whole affair was that No. 9 left La Salle St. about 4:00 am. Nearly six hours late, but he did have at least one RPO. You know, I don't recall receiving a lot of criticism for this incident or even hearing any more about it. If I hadn't been calling George every half hour and had he gotten to his office in the morning or got a call from "management" about what happened to No. 9, there would have been "guts on the moon" for everyone involved, specifically, as "Boss Hogg" used to say: "Namely me".

All of my "supererogatory efforts" took place while wearing the trainmaster's full dress uniform...i.e. suit, white shirt, tie, overcoat and felt hat. Nothing else would do. Many times I felt as I heard one roadmaster say...."We wear a suit just like a pair of overalls". Indeed for an operating officer to appear on the job not attired in a suit et al would have been as unlikely as a section man or trainman to appear without his overalls. Many a night I found myself crawling under an engine or boxcar with blocks or frogs while wearing suit and tie….It was a different world then.. When I see present day operating officers and even maintenance of way officers out and about in sport shirt and mackinaw, I think of how much more practical it would have been during my operating days, but it just wasn't done.

Thinking back (and filling up the rest of the page here) I am still going through boxes of files from the Fairbury Depot and just a couple of days ago I got into a box of really pretty good stuff. All of this was from the era when George Voss was Superintendent at Des Moines. In his earlier days, before I started with the RI in 1959 George had been transferred to a couple of other divisions, the Missouri Kansas and the Arkansas. During my brief tenure at Little Rock in 1961 one of the old timers there commented to me that "If Voss had been here another week, somebody would have killed him". George was returned to the Chicago Division, I think in about 1959 and all thought he would complete his career there "at home". But after the new management (Jervis Langdon and G. W. Kelly) arrived in 1964, George's star rose as they were impressed with his ability to get things done and change, where as most of the other old timers like B. F. Wells and B. R. Dew, and their protégés wouldn't change and were promptly sent packing into retirement.

George was sent to Des Moines in about 1966 as Supt. of the Des Moines Division which included much of what was the old Western Division with headquarters at Fairbury and hence the correspondence in the Fairbury Files. Reading the letter copies from George is literally like going back in time 40 years for me. I can hear and see him saying those things as though it were yesterday. One of George's most used sayings was "I MEAN TO SAY'...This preceded most of his general harangues. As I read copies of his correspondence he seemed to have changed a bit. His most used expression after opening volley was "WHAT I AM TRYING TO TELL YOU..." I guess this is equivalent to "I MEAN TO SAY"

Another of George's favorite things to do was to go into someone's territory...Discover something amiss...Telephone the officer in charge and shout "DID YOU KNOW HEDGPETH (or some other officer) THAT...."

IMPROVING OFFICE EFFICIENCY

The year was 1963. The Chicago Division Terminal Superintendent's office was a long, narrow, two story, brick and block building with a nearly true north-south orientation. It sat at the west edge of the Burr Oak yard, just south of the 127th St.. overpass.

At the north end of the building was a wooden stairway leading down from the second story to ground level and a stairway leading up to the street level of the overpass. At the

The author took this photograph of the Chicago Terminal Division Headquarters in 1990. The Rock Island ceased operations 10 years earlier.

south end was a stairway leading from ground level up to the second story.

On ground level the south end was occupied by the switchmen's locker room, and the north end by the in-freight yard office. Said yard office consisted of the usual bill and car record clerks, outside clerks, PPSI (Perishable Protective Service Inspectors) clerks, and various other functionaries. All of the messages, both inbound and outbound were handled through this office. Inbound and outbound waybills were sorted and processed here for deliveries from inbound connections and outbound trains. The usual yard office chaos and noise and horseplay were always happening. Clerks yelling at each other, trainmen and switchmen lounging about waiting for their engines to come off the coal track. All messages were transmitted via printers which were constantly clattering. All this punctuated by the continual ringing of the phones and shouted phone conversation. There's nothing like a yard office for concentrated insanity.

About 2/3 of the second story from the south end was occupied by the Superintendent's Office proper. The Super's private office was located at the extreme south end on the east wall. Northward along the east wall were located private offices of roadmaster, division engineer, signal supervisor and the Assistant Superintendent. Down the center of the second floor was an aisle-way formed by file cabinets located outside of the private offices on the east and the desks of the superintendent's clerks along the west wall. At the extreme south end on the west wall, just outside of the "Throne Room" sat Bill Perry, Chief Clerk to the Superintendent, just to his north sat the superintendent's secretary and to her north was a maintenance clerk and a couple of other clerical types, one of whom was "Smiley" Bettenhausen of the Bettenhausen racing family. Smiley was about 60 years old and had a surly disposition. Someone once said, "Smiley's the most even-tempered guy I've ever seen...mad all the time". Separating the south 2/3rds of the office occupied by the Superintendent's staff and the actual "nerve center" was a wall across the entire width of the building with a door in the center.

North of this wall, which was kind of flimsy wooden thing with translucent glass and a door in the center was the Trainmaster's office on the east side and the transportation clerk's desk on the west wall. The job of the transportation clerk was to answer the telephone and be the transmitter of all messages affecting the operation of the division. When you wanted to know anything about the operation, he was supposed to know the answer or at least know where to get it. He was supposed to keep the yardmaster and trainmaster apprised as to any difficulties which cropped up, which were many.

The trainmaster's office on the east side consisted of a desk where the TM was supposed to be when he wasn't chasing down some crisis, out re-railing a car or prodding a switch crew. There were several telephones, an intercom to the infreight and outfreight yard offices as well as a "tower intercom" where he could listen in to conversations between towers. The TM's desk faced the west directly at the transportation clerk's desk, so they could talk (shout) back and forth.

Because all of the messages came into the infreight yard office printers, it was necessary for all of the messages that affected the TM or Transportation Clerk to be hand carried out the north door of the downstairs office, outside, up the outside stairway and back into the north end of the building.

The constant cry of the transportation clerks and the clerks downstairs had been for someone to figure out a way to get the messages back and forth between the first and second floor without someone having to physically carrying them first outside and then upstairs. Remember that this was before copying machines, fax machines or telephone intercoms. If the transportation clerk wanted to talk to a clerk downstairs, he had to dial him up on the company phone and vice versa. This was also before the advent of the office coffee machine. Coffee was brought down from the White Castle up at the top of the hill toward Vincennes Avenue and downtown Blue Island, usually by the PPSI Clerk (he had wheels and probably had the least to do). The cry would go out that the PPSI was going for coffee. Everybody would order it to their liking. It took me a while to figure out what Boston (cream and sugar), Double Boston (two creams etc) was. George Voss was not an advocate of anyone drinking coffee in the office and maintained a vigilant watch for the PPSI making a coffee run. His campaign against coffee at the desk was a continuing one but it was a losing battle.

Now you have context as the newswriters say....I'll bet you wondered where this was all going???? Really nowhere, as none of this stuff does, but here's the story anyhow.

I came into work one evening...it was about 6:00 pm...I usually went up to the north end of the building to go in, if I thought that George was still around...the fewer encounters the better.... As I walked in said north door, there was George, the day trainmaster, assistant superintendent Frank Garner, and Cliff Brogden, the other night trainmaster. They were all standing around the transportation clerk's desk.

As I came in the door" George shouted at me. "Hedgpath... sic... come over here, I want to show you something". My first thought was, as usual, "What have I done now?".....But it was not me this time who was the "Target".

"Look at this" George yelled,.... "Just look at this". I looked and what did I see?... I saw directly beside the Transportation Clerk's chair a piece of heavy angle iron formed into an elongated S shape. The lower foot of the S was bolted to the floor beside a hole about 8 inches in diameter, which had been bored through the floor all the way through the ceiling of the office below. The upper horizontal leg of the S had, attached to it what appeared to be a clothesline pulley. Around said pulley was a piece of clothesline rope which had attached to one of its extremities a Karo syrup type bucket of about half gallon capacity like those farm kids used to take their lunch to school in. The other extremity of the rope led down though the hole and ended on a desk in the office below. We now had a device suitable to transmit documents from the lower office to the upper office without going outside.

George, however, was not pleased. "Look at that Hedgpeth"...he yelled again... "Now just look at that".... "You're an engineer....now is that engineering?".....He carried on at some length regarding the "engineering ability" of someone who could come up with something like that. That someone was the Division Engineer whose initials were TWT, but who was not on George's list of favorite people. I once heard it said by a colleague of TWT's... "T.... is blinded by his own radiance".

We all stood around the new "invention" for a few minutes and George continued his diatribe regarding TWT and this device. Just before he retreated to his office and hence his car to go home, he pointed his finger at the group and ended his rant with these words: "The first time I see a cup of coffee coming up in that thing, somebody's going to be in trouble!" He turned and stomped off in the direction of his office.

The rest of us stood around for a few minutes and watched while the invention was tried out by the transportation clerk. To add insult to injury the pulley squeaked whenever it was used, so there was no way to surreptitiously transmit any messages or contraband without detection. Cliff Brogden dubbed the new provider of office efficiency THE OLD OAKEN BUCKET. It was so referred to until its demise after a relatively short period of service. I believe that it was retired before I left Blue Island in April of 1964.

ASSET PROTECTION

I recently visited Kansas City, and while there took the opportunity to view the recently restored Union Station. It's a beautiful thing and well worth taking a look at there. The Kansas City Model Railroad Clubs were having weekend activities there and the various railroad historical societies are having displays. I had the chance to visit with a member of the Milwaukee Historical Society. He knew several former Rock Island men that I knew so we had a nice visit.

After we left the UD we headed down into the west bottoms. That's the area just down the bluff from KC proper where all the railroads had their freight houses. I had been wanting for sometime to take a look at the old Rock Island Freight House where we had our Salvage Store when I was Manager of Freight Claims. I had heard that there had been a fire and that most of the old Freight House had burned, but that the north end where the office was not completely destroyed and was being rebuilt. I found such to be the case.

The warehouse itself is gone and nothing is left but the concrete slab floor. The office at the north end which housed the Salvage Store at 14th and Wyoming is still there and appears to be in the process of restoration.

Looking at the two-story office structure brought back a memory...everything brings back a memory for me. Here it is:

The salvage store "retail office" consisted of a large room on the first floor which apparently had been the old freight office before the freight house was moved to the new office building Armourdale. There was a counter toward the south end of the room where the business was transacted. Because the store was open to the public, cash sales were made and considerable cash would sometimes be on hand behind the counter.

On the second floor of the building was the office of the Chief Special Agent for the Rock Island. I believe that the Division Special Agent also had his office there also.

It was installed long before I was on the scene, but someone had at one time decided that it would be a good idea to provide an alarm system in case of a holdup. Said alarm system consisted of a button on the floor behind the counter such that if there was "trouble" the person behind the counter could step on the button and it would ring a bell in the Special Agent's office upstairs and those boys could do the necessary. I think that banks have such a setup today.

Anyhow Bob McMahon, who was in charge of the store, when I was there told of an incident that happened even before he came there. It seems that one day, someone behind the counter inadvertently stepped on the alarm button and before anyone knew what was happening, several "Pussyfoots" came charging down the stairs from upstairs with guns drawn and ready to blast the errant intruder. Anyone familiar with the "Keystone Kops" image that railroad detectives had at the time will appreciate that incident.

YARDMASTER FOR A DAY

It was summer of 1963. I was working as one of the night assistant trainmasters in the Chicago Terminal. I had been "promoted" from Assistant TM at Joliet to Acting Trainmaster at Blue Island in the fall of 1962 after George Voss had suffered a heart attack that summer and everyone had been moved up a notch. George returned to duty sometime during

the spring or early summer of 1963 and all returned to their previous assignments.

Cliff Brogden and I were sharing the night duty at Blue Island and 12th St. I had been working the 12th St. assignment and Cliff was at Blue Island. I don't remember quite why Cliff was off, maybe on his 3 days off. As I said before, we got three days a month off back then. No that's not three days a week or three days in addition to weekends...that's just 3 days each month period. Prior to D. B. Jenks arrival at the Rock Island there were NO designated days off for operating officers and it was not unusual for an officer's vacation to be canceled because of an "emergency". George could create one at the drop of a hat. It was just like the military going on "alert"...all leaves were canceled.

To set the scene: I was working alone on the night trick: 6:00 pm to 6:00 am (on a short day). Most days it was 5:30 pm or so to 8:00-9:00 am or whenever George turned you loose after he had come in at 7:30 am or so and rehashed all of your mistakes and late trains from the night before and then told you to "go home and get your rest". I made the mistake once of saying "sleep fast huh?". That didn't set well with GHV and reflected a bad attitude on my part.

You may or may not be aware that yardmasters come from switchmen. The Blue Island day yardmaster job (7:00 am to 3:00 pm) was the hottest, most intense YM job on the division and probably anywhere on the system at that time. When the day yardmaster came to work, he was usually greeted by a very quiet scene, with only one engine out of about 5 or 6 which had started the night trick at 11:00 - 11:59 pm. These jobs were: House, Rip Track, Infreight, Outfreight, Englewood, and Coachyard. The outfreight engine (located in the outbound yard, directly under the yardmasters shack mounted on the 127th St. overpass) which almost never left the yard, was the hot job. It made up all of the outbound trains departing Blue Island. All of the other engines as mentioned were used up as the night wore on to make deliveries of perishable traffic off of the hotshot fruit and meat trains arriving in the wee morning hours with traffic for the IHB (Indiana Harbor Belt), B & O, Grand Trunk and the CPT (Chicago Produce Terminal), and Wood Street (potato terminal). The perishable trains started arriving at about 4:00 am with "cutoff" time of 4:30 am for the IHB. There would be 3-4 trains coming in and you had to decide whether you could get all of the perishables off all the trains into one delivery, or make more than one delivery and insure that the first couple would "make the connection". Whatever decision you made was sure to be wrong and second-guessed by George and "management". All of this does not relate directly to the topic at hand, but is only to illustrate that when the new day began at BI it was indeed a new day with the really hot stuff pressing you forward. The "really hot stuff" was the makeup and on time departure of No. 81 (Denver hotshot) and No. 91 (GSX) GOLDSTREAK with autos and auto parts for California. No. 81 was due out at 11:00 am and No. 91 was due out at 12:00.

As the day began there was nothing at all in the yard for

these trains. Everything came from eastern connections and were invariably late. The B & O would bring auto parts as would the IHB, hopefully early in the morning. The Wabash would deliver parts at a point north of Gresham, the CEI would deliver at Oakdale and there would be some stuff from the Pennsylvania at Englewood. The usual procedure was for the night engines who had made deliveries to pick up these connections on their way back from the deliveries and bring them to Blue Island. As the daylight YM viewed his no engine yard he could look both ways and gaze at a sea of headlights approaching from all directions, these being the foreign line deliveries approaching the yard. All the day YM had to do was sort out these 8-10 deliveries, making up No.'s 81 and 91 and

Left to right: Blue Island Trainmaster, Frank Vestal; Division Asst, Superintendent (and master re-railer) Frank Garner and George Voss. When these three had to attend a meeting "downtown," and after a night on duty, the author was given the responsibility of supervising an untried acting yardmaster. The trains got made up only thanks to another "supererogatory effort" by assistant trainmaster J. Pete Hedgepeth.

get them out on time. Bill O'Conner, who had been up and down the ladder of "officialdom" several times was the regular day man. Bill was a very competent and efficient YM, but was extremely nervous and tended to "loose his cookies" over the 127th St. bridge when the situation intensified. It was a "hot" job and everybody watched 81 and the Goldstreak.

As earlier mentioned, yardmasters come from switchmen. Working as afternoon outfreight engine foreman was a very short individual named George. (I am not going to otherwise designate him). George, was vertically challenged and tended to be, very "cocky" and had even told afternoon yardmaster Al Simnick (who I am told is still working for METRA) in the Chicago area) that he was a "Commander". We never figured out what he commanded, but Al and I always referred to him as "The Commander". "The Commander" was not even a good switchman let alone YM potential, but one day he decided that he wanted to be a yardmaster. Under the union rules you have to let anyone who wants to try it and then disqualify them if they don't make it.

The Commander (hereinafter referred to as C) spent a few days sitting in the yardmaster's shack with the various yardmasters. C was of the opinion that he really didn't need to break in and that he was just wasting his time, he was ready to take over. Al and I had a few laughs wondering what his first day would be like. Little did I know.........

It had been a rough night and I was ready to go home when Frank Garner (assistant Supt.) and Frank Vestal (trainmaster) walked into the Trainmaster's office. Frank Garner said "Well Jimmie (that's who I was at that time) George (C) is going to be day YM today. All of the operating officers at Blue Island (George Voss, Frank Vestal, Frank Garner) except you have to go downtown for a meeting. I guess you better stay here with George (C)." My heart (and soul) crashed to my feet. There was nothing I could do.

I "girded up my loins" and went over the bridge to see what C was doing. As I walked in, there he was trying to operate the console which controlled the yard speaker system, the radio, and the tower communication system. He didn't have a clue. He finally was able to answer an engine coming down track five with a long string containing auto parts etc. which would have to be sorted out for 81 and the GSX. After he finally figured out how to talk to the engine he finally told them to come down track 43. Track 43 was the track we made the outbound trains up on. I asked George why he was bringing him down 43? He, of course, didn't know. I let him go for a few minutes and after he started a couple of other moves which would have resulted in disaster, I finally decided that I couldn't do any worse than he was going to do. I said get out of the chair George.... I'll do it. Now I have never been anything close to a switchman, never mind a competent switchman and never a yardmaster, but I figured it's "do or die" today!

It was a hot summer day, the AC was cooling the shanty, but the sweat poured off of me in rivers as I, without help, encouragement or supervision oversaw the makeup of 81 and

Yardmaster Bill O'Conner looks a bit stressed in this ROCKET cover shot as he communicates with his yard crews in this 1963 photograph.

The author played "yardmaster for a day" after a switchman was given a chance to tryout for the YM job and made a real mess of things

the "Streak" No. 81 got out before noon, which was about par for the course. The GSX followed No. 3 (The Golden State due out of La Salle St. at 1:00 pm) which wasn't "standard" but quite often happened.

About 12:30 or so Frank Garner called from "downtown" to see how things were. I told him that I had taken over and I really don't remember whether C stayed around or not. We never heard any more from C about being a yardmaster.

I went home about 2:00 pm as emotionally drained as I have ever been. There was no question of going to bed to rest up for night duty. (There was no compensatory time off for such extra duty).

That experience was one of those which you wouldn't do again for a million dollars, but wouldn't take a million dollars for the education. I got a great deal of personal satisfaction out

of the deal and the Rock Island didn't suffer too badly with late trains that day. It truly was one for the book.

All the guys who baled out on me that day had a good laugh, and of course there was no special commendation from George Voss or "management" for my "supererogatory" service. There really is such a word, but I can't get it spelled. All I got from George was "I mean to say how come you couldn't get 91 out ahead of No. 3. How will I explain that to management?"

The rest of the experience has faded into the shadows of the past. The "Commander" will, however always remain a vivid memory.

A RAT OF A DIFFERENT COLOR

I don't know why, but recently I thought of another bit of trivia which I don't believe I have memorialized here before...When I do put it down now...you'll think, rightfully so. "That guy has just got too much time on his hands"...

ANYHOW.........................

At the time I first went to the Chicago Division in 1961 the railroad was reaping big benefits from J. D. Farrington's purchase of the Pullman Railroad in about 1950. This line ran south from Pullman Junction...A very interesting place, through the Calumet Industrial District, past a large Sherwin Williams Paint factory about 115th and down to Lake Calumet Harbor where ships from foreign countries would unload their cargos after coming in from Atlantic Ocean, through the Saint Lawrence Seaway and down Lake Michigan to Cal Harbor Terminal. There was a tremendous business going at that time, although it had started to slack off a bit by the time I arrived.

South of Sherwin Williams was a new yard which the Rock Island had constructed to hold the backed up grain and steel business which overflowed from Cal Harbor Terminal...There, of course, was always grain on the ground. In addition, at that time, the City of Chicago was still dumping raw garbage as fill in the Lake Calumet area. Every night a "garbage run" brought gondolas of "stuff" from the various collection points around the south side of Chicago. I don't remember what Railroad gave us the cars, may have been the BRC... Anyhow. With a continual trail of garbage from Pullman Jct. south, as well as the huge dump plus the grain guess what flourished in great abundance.....RATS lots of RATS....BIG RATS....running everywhere.

It became a sport of the employees of the Sherwin Williams Plant to spray any rodent which came in range of their location. We had red rats, silver rats, yellow rats, green rats and perhaps a few other colors chasing along the right of way and through the industries. Just another "great Rock Island Memory."

As a footnote, and a sad one, *TRAINS* magazine carried an article describing the destruction of the old Pullman Company General Office building .The fire was apparently arson in nature started by a disgruntled employee. The Rock Island, through the Pullman Railroad, served this facility and the area is undergoing a rebirth. The old Florence Hotel as well as the

Cal-Sag Harbor where grain was transloaded to ships from the R.I.

town of Pullman, the original "company town" is being restored. As the Pullman area is undergoing a revitalization. How sad to see a historic structure destroyed in a senseless act.

When I was first at Blue Island and then was later assigned to South Chicago, the Pullman yard was literally crammed full of heavyweight Pullman's awaiting disposition or a call to further duty which never came. These cars gradually disappeared, until by the mid 1970's they were all gone...Away to their final "line".

SNOW BROOMS ILLUSTRATED

Safely working "downtown" by 1967, Pete Hedgpeth missed all the fun of digging out Burr Oak Yard from a record snowfall. Burr Oak was flat-switched (no hump). An Alco C-415 and many Rock Islanders are hard at work getting the yard operational.

In a December issue of *TRAINS* the winter photo section features three great photos of railroading in the wintertime. One photo on page shows a CNW employee thawing switch points with a FUSEE. Still the old reliable method when there are no switch heaters. Photo at bottom of the same page shows two crewmen cleaning switchpoints. One appears to be using the chisel point which most brooms had on the broom-handle end opposite the bristles to clear the points and the other is attempting to unlock the lock on the ground throw "high star" switch stand with his broom "at the ready'. They have made some progress on the points, but still have some work to do to get the bridal rod and connecting rods freed up.

CHRISTMAS AT BLUE ISLAND

My thoughts have drifted back to Christmases past which were spent in humble servitude to G. H. Voss at Blue Island Terminal. George never wanted to recognize any holiday or even Sundays....We were expected to be on duty for the full term every hour of every day other than on our "days off".. (at that time it was three each month). In either 1962 or 63 Frank Garner came to BI as Assistant Terminal Superintendent. Frank was an Arkansawer and had previously been Trainmaster at Council Bluffs. Frank was an excellent railroader and was about as different from George as it was possible to be. Cliff Brogden and I referred to him as "Local Chairman for the Trainmasters". Ralph Parker who had been Terminal Trainmaster at Blue Island forever and was continually locked in mortal combat with George, consequently never had any authority to change any of George's policies, had been transferred and Frank was a "new broom" and George put him in charge of arranging the days off for the officers.

Since George had required that there be two trainmasters on duty every night no matter what, Frank let Cliff and I arrange for one of us to take part of the night off on Saturday nights after we had both come on duty at the appointed time and gotten No. 59 (the piggyback train) out and assuming all was quiet otherwise. This was not to be communicated to George and it usually worked pretty well.

Came Christmas of 1963 and Frank Garner called all of us TM's in. Frank Vestal, Cliff Brogden and I and said that we would work out a "shift" arrangement for Christmas Day so that all of us could have some time at home. One guy came in at midnight Christmas Eve, he went home in the morning and someone else came in about 8:00 am and stayed until about noon, then someone else came in at noon and stayed until early evening and then someone else from early evening through the night. I don't remember which shift I drew, but it worked OK. I was told that George, as was expected, called repeatedly throughout the day and every time he did he was talking to a different TM, but it all seemed to work out with no ill effects.

Winter railroading is not fun anywhere, but on the South Side of Chicago the winters of 62-63 and 63-64 were particularly miserable. I can remember many occasions lying on my back (in my suit and overcoat) trying to thaw a suburban coach or re-rail a car or engine. I was never any good at re-railing and usually gave up after making a few tries and making the situation worse. Frank Garner was a "master re-railer". He always walked around with his hands in his pockets with his suit coat buttoned. He would get someone to throw down a few blocks and an old angle bar or two with a couple of track spikes. Frank, with his hands never coming out of his pockets, would kick the blocks around with his feet and then say "try it now"....a little pull and the car or engine would jump right back on. "Some have got it and some haven't."

Russ Carl, the signal supervisor, was assigned a company vehicle which was a Bronco or whatever the forerunner of the Bronco was. Kind of a jeep vehicle. It had a company radio and something which resembled a heater, but didn't do much. It had no windshield washers. Someone had the bright idea that Russ should leave his machine parked at the terminal office for the Trainmasters to use at night, thus saving paying us TM's car mileage or having an additional company car. Russ was less than thrilled with his arrangement. He had previously been able to use vehicle to drive back and forth to home, but was now not able to do so. It was a constant hassle as to who was to maintain the car, keep the gas tank filled etc.

The vehicle company number escapes me now (George's car was 84 and we would often comment "Car 84 where are you?...remember the old TV show Car 54 where are you)....Anyhow, Russ's jeep in addition to having a minimally effective heater, additionally possessed a minimally effective generator. Often during the cold winter nights we would be sitting in this vehicle out on "the hill" watching the IHB "takeoff"... (Pulling the perishables off the rear end of 84, 82 DCX and shoving them down to the IHB)... With the engine idling, the heater running, and the company radio on, the battery would go down and when the engine was shut off it wouldn't restart.

The crowning moment of Russ's frustration and wrath and yelling at George about the vehicle use arrangement came one winter morning, when he went out to get in the vehicle and found: the battery dead, the gas tank nearly empty and one of the tires flat. I had already left for home when Russ marched into George's office, but reliable sources reported that the sight and sound was glorious.

Needless to say the Trainmasters received a scathing letter from George regarding the situation, which we promptly tossed into the trash along with 90% of the other stuff which found its way into our mailboxes.

As I have related in previous diatribes, it seemed that the worse the winter, the heavier business became. Spring seemed so far removed from the day-by-day situation, that the daily routine of 12-16 hour days 7 days every week and a daily chastisement from George, that railroading had changed for me from a highly sought after career to nearly a prison confinement. I screwed up my courage one day and went into see George regarding my "situation" and how long I was going to be "permanent night trainmaster" at Blue Island. My interview with George provided about as much information for me as did Clinton's grand jury interview for them. I left thinking..." now what did he say"?

A few days later I went downtown and interviewed with an

Executive Search firm, but before anything came of that, I received a phone call from John Gilfillan inquiring as to whether I would be interested in a job in the Freight Claims Department... I was, and after the interview he sent a letter to George asking him to release me ASAP for duty in the Claims department.

The man who could heretofore do nothing right in George's eyes, suddenly became "the most valuable man on the division"...and the story of his stalling and delaying my release could have given the Clinton Whitehouse a few ideas on delay tactics.

At the recent Train Show my annual quest for new-old RAILROAD and TRAINS magazines was richly rewarded as I stumbled onto a virtual "mother lode" of 1960's and 70's RR magazines at a very reasonable price. I was able to find several complete years bundled and ready to go. Since I do have one or two other obligations, even at my advanced stage of life (borderline dotage) I haven't even done anything but skim through a couple of year's worth and glean out a few issues with Harry Bedwell and E. S. Dellinger tales. This is my primary reason for seeking these back issues. There are a couple of other nuggets in some of the issues, one of which I'll relate here since I was somewhat directly involved. The Mail Car section of the August 1975 issue of RAILROAD carried a little article entitled: "Brass Collars Fired."

This little gem opened with a commentary on John Ingram's somewhat famous reference to "the Madison Hotel Gang"...This was brought about by executives of several, if not all, of Rock Island's competitors sitting down in the Madison Hotel and dividing up the Rock Island among themselves. Ingram stated that "Of course the body they were dividing up was still alive, "he pointed out, emphasizing that: (1) the Rock Island is still in operation; (2) there is no immediate threat to its future operations, and (3) the Rock (I hate that term) needs a major overhaul and a full measure of understanding help from shippers.

Prior to this statement, the bankrupt Rock Island had trimmed 200 managerial jobs from its executive ladder in a new move to conserve cash and regain a financial footing. The system-wide dismissals covered officials in positions ranging from vice president to computer analyst, 60 of the positions eliminated being in Chicago.

I remember the situation vividly. It was in May of 1975 to my best recollection. I was, at that time, in the Industrial Development Department with the title of Assistant General Industrial Agent. John Kirtley, earlier famous for his "we're just not equipped for prosperity comment" had been recently named Director of Industrial Development and Real Estate. John called me in one day and told me that there was going to be wholesale layoffs in the management ranks. He said that he expected to be among the missing, but thought that I might survive. I was headed out of town that day for an Industrial Development Conference someplace in downstate Illinois near Saint Louis. I asked John if I should cancel my plans. He told me to just go ahead and do what I had planned. He said, "Call me at home tomorrow night, and we'll know what happened".

The next evening after the conference, with great fear and trepidation, I called John. His first words to me were. "Well, you're the only one left," John's job had been eliminated and he was transferred back to the Freight Sales Department from whence he had come. All of the Industrial Representatives at the various locations across the system were out as were some of the office real estate people. Talk about your weeping, wailing and gnashing of teeth....It was bad.

The operating department engaged in a great "smoke and mirrors" operation....shuffling people all around, but in the end actually cutting almost no jobs. They seemed to be able to convince Ingram and the Trustee that they had actually done something, but in reality they had done almost nothing, but created a great cloud of dust and obfuscation. The wailing in our department mostly consisted of "how come the operating department can get away with really eliminating no jobs and we're losing ours".

Many of the jobs eliminated should have been eliminated much earlier. In the halcyon days of the Langdon era departments and jobs had been added helter-skelter an example was the Piggyback Department. Management just brought in a guy named Frank Sutherland, who had been head of a trucking company and created a whole new department, consisting mostly of "truck drivers with neckties on" who were busily engaged in taking business out of boxcars and putting it in TOFC. It was wild while it lasted. Ingram, in one fell swoop, eliminated this bloated monster and several others which should never have existed in the first place.

The Hatchet Falls

I survived another two and one half years, knowing that the hatchet was going to get me eventually, not knowing just when. We weren't doing any Industrial Development work, and given the Rock Island's circumstances in 1975 and later, few industries were clamoring for Rock Island locations.

My day came January 28, 1978. My boss then was R. L. Ferguson. He called me in one afternoon and I could tell by the look on his face that the news wasn't good. He said "Your job is eliminated January 31st. You are supposed to contact Hoenig (W. C. Hoenig, then General Manager) and see about a job in the operating department.

I thought about the situation as I rode home on the suburban train in blinding snowstorm. The weather matched my disposition.

I did talk with Bill Hoenig who painted an unrealistic picture of the situation for me. He said "why don't you go out and visit with Charlie Pitts, then Terminal Superintendent at Blue Island and we'll make you Trainmaster there and soon we'll be needing some superintendents etc. etc. etc. I did go over and visit with Charlie, who had been a yardmaster at South Chicago when I was train-mastering at Blue Island 15 years before. The weather and the conditions were just like they had been when I left, and after visiting with Charlie I thought that I really didn't want to go back to where I had been 15 years earlier. I also wondered if Hoenig would be there much longer also. Those pre-Ingram managers were dropping rapidly. I decided that I really didn't want to stick around so I told Bill Hoenig, "thanks but no thanks"... My hunch was right...Within 6 months Hoenig had departed for the SP and I would not have had a mentor. For the first and only time in my life I filed for unemployment benefits with the Railroad Retirement Board....It was then $135 weekly. I drew that for a month or so and then got into the real estate business.

Many of the guys I knew and worked with stayed around and hung on even after the shutdown in 1980 and worked for the trustee. My good friend Jim Beatty whom I worked with in the Claims Department went to the IHB as head of their personnel department and retired 4-5 years ago. He is about the only former RI person I am in contact with. It was an interesting nearly 20 years.

Earlier you saw a couple of photos of George Voss and he had a standard expression when things went wrong, and he was seeking someone to blame. He would say in an accusing tone: "What am I going to tell management"?.....Or: "How can I explain this to management?" When these statements were made I often wondered whether George considered himself a part of management?

Once, it is said, in a Division Staff Meeting, George, after relating some blunder on someone's part, asked the usual.... "What am I going to tell management?" It was reportedly said that Joe Salapatek, Blue Island Rip Track Foreman (cover) commented: "You could tell them you're sorry".

George's response was not made a part of the record.

#####

Printed in the United States
61754LVS00004B/297